SPACE TRAVELERS

An Interactive Program for Developing
Social Understanding, Social Competence
and Social Skills for Students with
Asperger Syndrome, Autism and
Other Social Cognitive Challenges

Space Guide Manual

SPACE TRAVELERS

An Interactive Program for Developing Social Understanding, Social Competence and Social Skills for Students with Asperger Syndrome, Autism and Other Social Cognitive Challenges

Space Guide Manual

M. A. Carter and J. Santomauro
Foreword by Jeanie McAfee

Autism Asperger Publishing Co.
P.O. Box 23173
Shawnee Mission, KS 66283-0173
www.asperger.net

P.O. Box 23173
Shawnee Mission, KS 66283-0173
www.asperger.net

© 2004 by Autism Asperger Publishing Company
P.O. Box 23173
Shawnee Mission, KS 66283-0173
www.asperger.net

Publisher's Cataloging-in-Publication
(Provided by Quality Books, Inc.)

Carter, M. A.
   Space travelers : an interactive program for developing social understanding, social competence and social skills for students with AS, autism and other social cognitive challenges : space guide manual / M.A. Carter and J. Santomauro.
      p. cm.
      Includes bibliographical references.
      LCCN 2004111386
      ISBN 1-93-1282-61-7

   1. Social skills in children--Study and teaching.
2. Social perception in children. 3. Asperger's syndrome--Patients--Education. 4. Autistic children--Education.
I. Santomauro, J. (Josie) II. Title.

HQ783.C37 2004   302'.14'071
                                  QBI04-800041

This book is designed in Postino Italic and Tekton

Managing Editor: Kirsten McBride
Editorial Support: Ginny Biddulph

Printed in the United States of America

We appreciate ...

School communities that participated in the *Space Travelers* pilot program:

- St. Peter Chanel, Australia
- Our Lady of Dolours, Australia
- Our Lady of the Assumption, Australia

We dedicate ...

Space Travelers is designed to make a difference in the lives of children who have difficulty understanding and being successful in the social world. Many children we have come across in our professional lives find social interactions perplexing, frustrating and infuriating. They have difficulty establishing connectedness with others, let alone sustaining it. Their repertoire of competencies in navigating the social world is often sparse and frequently inappropriately executed. They require support in learning more constructive ways of creating and retaining successful social connections with others. It is for this purpose that we wrote this program.

We dedicate this program to children across the globe as they strive towards developing their competencies as social individuals, not only in their world as students in contemporary times but as leaders of the world tomorrow.

– M. A. Carter and J. Santomauro

TABLE OF CONTENTS

FOREWORD

I had the pleasure of meeting Josie Santomauro while I was studying with Tony Attwood in Brisbane in the spring of 2000. At that time, Josie had already authored a series of refreshingly up-beat booklets for children with autism spectrum disorders, their parents, and the professionals working with these very special children. In *Space Travelers*, Josie and co-author, Margaret Carter, have put together an easy-to-follow curriculum for an eight-session course in social-emotional skills for mid-grade school-aged children with Asperger Syndrome, higher functioning autism and related disorders. *Space Travelers* comes as a set containing both a teacher's manual and a student workbook.

The curriculum will work as either a brief introduction to social-emotional skills and anger management for children with autism spectrum disorders or, alternatively, as a complete course for children who are not on the spectrum but need help with social-emotional skills. It focuses on social problem solving and emotion management — both of which are key deficit areas for children with social-cognitive challenges.

Space Travelers is user-friendly, employing the same easy-to-use format in each of the eight lessons. The classes last 1-1/2 — 2 hours each, and are packed with activities that include written assignments, role-plays, guided imagery, conversational exchanges, games, arts, and crafts. The group leader may tailor the classes to the group with which he or she is working by choosing from several activities offered with each lesson. Weekly home handouts ensure that parents or guardians are informed of the goals and activities for each session. Teachers complete journal entries after each lesson to record what went well and what could be improved to help them structure future classes. Students also record their positive experiences in a journal after each session. The teacher's guide contains several handouts and templates that book owners may reproduce for use in their classes. All of the activities may be carried out with minimal preparation, and the needed supplies are inexpensive and easy to obtain. The many entertaining visual prompts are designed to appeal to young children with autism spectrum disorders, most of whom are visual learners.

Space Travelers is based on a series of eight fun and imaginative "space missions" in which students take the roles of space travelers and the teacher is the space guide. To mention a few highlights, Mission 2 includes several practical but creative "getting to know you" types of questions that students use to interview one another. This activity gives students practice in two-way conversations and finding a topic of interest to a conversational partner, and promotes generalization by providing scripts that students can

use later in real-life conversations. At the end of this activity, space travelers have a chance to mime their answers to the scripted questions In a fun variation of the game of charades. Another activity in Mission 2, Star Qualities, uses visual prompts to aid students in giving compliments to themselves and to each other. The authors use cartooning, art, and role-play in Mission 3 to help students explore positive vs. negative thinking. Students work on theory-of-mind skills (the ability to understand what another person is thinking, feeling, or intending) in Missions 3 and 4 using the media of cartooning, drawing, and writing. Missions 4, 5 and 6 help students to expand their emotional vocabularies, deal with anger, and work on problem solving in social contexts. In Mission 7 the students review previous lessons and work on organizational skills, teamwork, collaboration, and negotiation skills while they plan for an end-of-course party held during Mission 8.

Space Travelers will make a valuable addition to the library of anyone who cares for or works with young children with high-functioning autism, Asperger Syndrome, pervasive developmental disorders-not otherwise specified, nonverbal learning disabilities, or other social-cognitive challenges. Its refreshing and fun approach to teaching social-emotional skills will appeal to children in grades three through five, and the book will be a welcome tool for any teacher or caregiver who needs a well-organized, easy-to-implement curriculum in this complex subject area.

> — Jeanie McAfee, M.D.
> Author, *Navigating the Social World*,
> Founder and Director, Social Solutions
> Fall 2004

INDUCTION

What Is Social Understanding?

We spend most of our lives living as members of social groups. The success we have in these groups is primarily determined by the quality of our social interactions, and these interactions are directly influenced by our social understanding skills and competencies. For many children, including those on the autism spectrum, social interactions with peers and adults create daily challenges. These children have a narrow repertoire of social problem-solving skills and competencies and a limited understanding of the reality of social situations, including the most appropriate way to respond in a given social context.

To illustrate, let us look at the following example involving a baseball game at recess.

Tim wants to have a turn batting before the recess bell rings. Jessie is batting at the moment, and when he is out, it will be Tim's turn. Tim is worried that he will not get a turn to bat and is getting angry that he has spent most of recess time waiting for his teammates to bat. He thinks it is stupid that you are not out until you are struck out. Tim wants his turn NOW!

This creates a social problem for Tim. It is Jessie's turn, not Tim's, and the rules of the game are very clear: You are not out just because one of your teammates wants to bat. You are out when you have been struck out.

Tim runs over to Jessie and begins shouting at him in a threatening voice: "You stop batting now! I want my turn. It's not fair. You always bat and I never get a turn. I want a turn NOW. Give me the bat!! Tim grabs the bat out of Jessie's hands and pushes him to the ground.

Jessie looks shocked and surprised. "What's the matter, Tim?" he asks. "I was following the rules." Jessie gets up and quietly says to Tim, "Come on, you know the rules. Go and wait until I get out."

Tim glares at Jessie and begins jumping up and down, hitting the air with his fist and shouting, "No, I won't. You aren't my friend. You are mean and horrible. I never want to play baseball again."

Jessie calls after Tim, "Hey, Tim. Wait up; you can play when it is your turn." Tim shouts back, "Never. Can't you read my lips? NEVER, NEVER, NEVER."

As illustrated, Tim has narrow repertoires of dealing with and expressing his frustrating and angering emotions. His behaviors are unhelpful and inappropriate and will not help him get a turn any sooner. In fact, quite the opposite. Tim would benefit from expanding his repertoire of constructive responses to social situations so that when things do not go the way he wants them to, he can deal with it in a more positive way. He needs to develop his social competencies and associated skills, both within the given social context and across contexts, and be supported in learning and internalizing them.

As this example shows, children, especially those with autism spectrum disorders (ASD) and other social cognitive challenges, need to be taught and consistently coached in using a range of strategies directed at broadening their social understanding skills and competencies so that their comprehension of and response to interpersonal interactions are more constructive and positive. This involves learning rational ways of living and working together in social situations and developing a more realistic understanding of the conventions of and the complexities associated with interacting with others within the social world. Being successful when engaging with others is dependent on social cognition, social skills, social competence and social understanding.

About This Book

Space Travelers is an eight-mission program based on a space journey theme for students in the middle elementary-school years, approximately grades 4 and 5. Briefly, the content is designed to introduce, develop and refine children's social understanding, social skills and social competencies in navigating the social world. By following the constellation chart (see page 14), the Space Guide (teacher or other facilitator) plots the journey for the Space Travelers (students), concluding with touchdown back on planet earth.

The purpose is for the Space Travelers to journey together through the galaxy, stopping at designated mission points to develop and refine their social skills and competencies. Once a mission is complete, the Space Travelers move on together to the next mission point, further consolidating and practicing their awareness and understanding of team travel.

Targeted areas include:

- social cognition and social understanding
- self-esteem and self-acceptance
- recognizing and respecting diversity
- understanding emotions, feelings and thinking patterns
- reflective problem solving
- stress release
- dealing with bullying behaviors
- goal setting and self-mastery
- self-regulation

Individuals with ASD experience significant difficulties understanding the social world, which in turn has the potential to create significant problems for them in terms of making and maintaining relationships with peers (e.g., Attwood, 1998). Successful social problem solving is often an enigma to these children, as are keeping calm, positive self-talk and teamwork. It is important that we teach children with ASD these concepts and the accompanying skills so that they continue to broaden their repertoire of social understanding and social competence. The *Space Travelers* program is written for this exact purpose — to help students with social cognitive deficits, including ASD, learn constructive social interaction skills in the area of social problem solving and emotion management.

How to Use This Book

The program is conducted during school time. It is facilitated by a classroom teacher, resource teacher, school administrator or school counselor in whole classes or in small groups of children (minimum of eight children). In addition, a newsletter (Mother Ship Update) outlining each mission is provided for home, in an effort to ensure that children have an opportunity to transfer their learning across home and school contexts.

The program is divided into eight missions that follow a similar format: Mission Ahead, constellation chart, core activities, Asteroid Asks, space journals, and Mother Ship Update. Each mission has a specific purpose, and the accompanying core activities are geared to this purpose. It is important that you as the Space Guide are clear about the purpose of why you are doing each activity and that you communicate this information to the children.

The time allocated for each mission is one and a half hours, except for Missions 1, 6 and 8, which are each two hours long. The eight missions can be taught over a semester (once a week) or half a semester (twice a week). The time may have to be adjusted depending on the needs of group members. For example, there may be missions where you complete every core activity and others where you choose to complete only two or three core activities. This may be because additional activities are necessary to fully teach a concept, because students' time on task is declining, and so on. However, while Space Guides have flexibility in terms of the number of core activities they choose to complete, we recommend that you complete a minimum of two activities for each mission.

Consider the following when planning your group sessions:

- Group size
- Group composition
- Group cohesion
- Time of day for session
- Academic engagement time of group members
- Suitability of mission itinerary for group members
- Need for paraprofessional (or other adult) support
- Availability of adult support
- Length of the session
- Frequency of the sessions

You may find it necessary to modify, adapt or change aspects of the program in response to the unique needs of individual children, thus ensuring that all children achieve success.

Space Traveler Manual

The accompanying Space Traveler manual is a unique component of this interactive program. It helps students stay on track and provides a way to keep their completed activities together. As such, the Space Traveler manuals also serve as an important review and assessment tool.

Missions Overview

The following outline shows the main purpose of each of the eight missions that make up the space journey.

1. **LAUNCH PAD** – The Space Guide introduces the purpose of the journey to the Space Travelers using the constellation chart.

2. **INTRODUCING THE CREW** – The Space Travelers recognize, develop and articulate their strengths, abilities, interests and areas of need.

3. **STARLIGHT AND GRAVITY THINKING** – The Space Travelers are introduced to helpful rather than unhelpful ways of thinking.

4. **THE FEELINGS SHUTTLE** – The Space Travelers' emotions vocabulary is introduced and expanded.

5. **ATMOSPHERIC PRESSURE** – The Space Travelers explore angry thinking, and angry feelings and actions in more detail and look at appropriate ways to deal with them.

6. **MISSION CONTROL** – The Space Travelers are introduced to reflective problem solving.

7. **SPACE WALKING – PREPARING FOR LANDING** – The Space Travelers continue to learn various relaxation techniques and prepare for touchdown.

8. **TOUCHDOWN PARTY** – Everybody celebrates and reflects on the Space Travelers' journey.

Success Stories

Space Guides and Space Travelers who have successfully piloted the Space Travelers program wrote the following testimonials.

Space Guides

- "I feel the program was worthwhile; the children learned new skills and communicated freely."

- "The children were enthusiastic about the program and would recommend it to other classes."

- "Children really absorbed the 'Starlight and Gravity' ways of thinking and have incorporated the language into their classroom language when describing behaviors and attitudes."

- "The children took to the program and were very willing to contribute."

- "We are very open with positives and negatives, and it is all very beneficial."

- "The children thoroughly enjoyed the program."

Space Travelers

- "It helped me to control my anger."

- "It helped me work well with others."

- "I learned to be a better friend."

- "I learned that thinking bad things is unhelpful."

- "It helped me to have fun without getting into trouble."

- "It helped me to think the right way."

- "I learned there are lots of different things to do if you are angry or upset."

- "I learned different people have different ways to deal with problems."

- "I learned always to look on the bright side of things."

- "I learned to believe in myself."

- "I learned I could fix my own problems by just saying 'sorry' and not fighting."

- "I learned how to help others when they are hurt."

- "I learned how to relax."
- "I learned how to control my feelings."
- "I learned to just walk away from bad things."
- "I learned how to communicate with other people in a helpful way."
- "I learned how to stay calm."
- "I learned everybody has feelings, not just me."
- "I learned to always be a starlight."
- "I learned how to get along and feel happy."
- "I learned how to understand my feelings and others' too."
- "I learned how to listen better."
- "I learned how to be kind to people."
- "I learned about working in a team."
- "I learned to never give up."
- "I learned how to listen better."

PREPARING FOR THE JOURNEY

Your Role as Space Guide

The Space Guide is the facilitator of the *Space Travelers* program. The role of Space Guide may be played by classroom teachers, resource teachers, administrators or school counselors. Guides may be supported by paraprofessionals, including teacher aides, parents and student teachers. We do not recommend giving paraprofessionals the role of Space Guide unless they are trained in using the material and mentored as they teach the program.

Your role as Space Guide is to guide the Space Travelers through their eight-mission social understanding journey. This involves familiarizing yourself with the missions before you begin the program, preparing yourself before each mission, maintaining regular communication with parents/guardians, creating an appropriate teaching and learning environment, teaching the missions, supporting and encouraging the Space Travelers in their learning, and reviewing and reflecting on the growth and development of each Space Traveler throughout the program.

Each mission consists of five activities. The missions are outlined in the Space Traveler manual, the student companion volume that is an important part of the program.

Scheduling the Journey

The content of each space mission is built upon the previous mission. Therefore, it is imperative that the missions are taught in the sequence in which they are presented here.

The time allocated for each mission is one and a half hours except for Missions 1, 6 and 8, which are each two hours long. The eight missions can be taught over a semester (once a week) or half a semester (twice a week).

Composition of groups is a school decision, either across grade level/s, small group (minimum 8*), or whole class.

If students with complex needs are part of the group, this minimum number may be reduced.

Mother Ship Lift-Off

Before you start the program, permission and support may need to be obtained from a number of people, which may include the following:

- parents/guardians
- school administrators
- classroom teacher
- learning support/inclusion teacher

If you require written permission from parents/guardians for students to participate in the *Space Travelers* program, you will find a sample letter on the next page. This letter may be photocopied onto school letterhead or used as a starting point to create your own letter.

Space Guide Itinerary

When planning your itinerary, be prepared to schedule the eight missions over the course of one semester.

The following is included in each mission within this manual:

1. *Space Guide's Maintenance Checklist*
2. *Space Travelers' Mission Outline*
3. *Mission Activities*
4. *Mother Ship Update*
5. *Space Guide Journal*

Constellation Chart

To assist you in guiding the Space Travelers with their missions, a pictorial constellation chart naming the eight missions is provided on page 14. Use this constellation chart as a point of reference at the beginning of each mission to identify the relation of the current mission to previous ones in terms of purpose, growth, and so on.

Enlarge the chart to poster size and display it in the classroom throughout the journey.

Note: When you see this astronaut throughout the manual, take note. He alerts you to important information.

Dear Parent/Guardian,

Next semester we will be running a small-group/whole-class social understanding program called *Space Travelers*. The program is directed towards supporting children in further developing and refining their understanding of social situations and assisting them in being successful in the social world.

Space Travelers consists of eight 1-1/2-hour group sessions, all of which will be conducted during school time. Topics to be explored during these sessions include: helpful ways of behaving in social situations, social problem solving and cooperative teamwork. Your child's classroom teacher/resource teacher will facilitate the program.

I am writing to invite your child to participate in the *Space Travelers* program. Please discuss this with your child. Please sign the permission slip below if you are both agreeable to your child's involvement in this program. Please return your signed form to the school on or before _____.

The *Space Travelers* program begins on _____ and concludes on _____. If you have any questions before, during or after the program, please contact me by telephone/fax, or e-mail as follows: _____

Yours Sincerely,
Space Guide
(Name)

SPACE TRAVELERS

I _____ give my child,

_____, permission to

participate in the Space Travelers program. By giving permission,

I also agree to support the school and the program by discussing

the space mission with my child at home.

Signed _____

MOTHER SHIP

Constellation Chart

MISSION 1

LAUNCH
PAD

MISSION 5

ATMOSPHERIC
PRESSURE

MISSION 2

INTRODUCING
THE CREW

MISSION 6

MISSION
CONTROL

MISSION 3

STARLIGHT AND
GRAVITY THINKING

MISSION 7

SPACE WALKING –
PREPARING FOR LANDING

MISSION 4

THE FEELINGS
SHUTTLE

MISSION 8

TOUCHDOWN
PARTY

From Carter, M., & Santomauro, J. (2004). Space travelers. Shawnee Mission, KS: Autism Asperger Publishing Company. Copied with permission.

LAUNCH PAD
SPACE GUIDE'S
MAINTENANCE CHECKLIST

MISSION AHEAD

Your goals as Space Guide for Mission 1 are to introduce and familiarize the Space Travelers with the purpose of the eight-week space journey, the constellation chart, their role in the overall mission and tasks specific to Mission 1. This is the foundation mission, preparing the whole team with the necessary equipment (i.e., constellation chart, rocket fuel tank, space journal) they will require for the whole journey. Space Travelers will be introduced to, taught and asked to commit themselves to the space contract team rules they are to follow during each mission.

MISSION OUTCOMES

Space Travelers will:

- ☐ Know the purpose of the journey
- ☐ Become familiar with the eight-week journey
- ☐ Be introduced to the sequence for each mission: constellation chart, space contract, core activities for the mission, Asteroid Asks, space journals, and Mother Ship Update

MISSION LENGTH

As this is the introductory mission, it is important to set time aside to allow the Space Travelers to explore and absorb all information pertaining to the eight missions. For this purpose, we recommend a time frame of at least two hours (this can be extended over two sessions if preferred) so as to allow the Space Travelers time to enjoy and prepare themselves for the journey ahead.

MISSION SUPPLIES

You will need the following:

- ☐ Space Traveler manual (one copy per Space Traveler)
- ☐ Decorative materials appropriate to the space theme (e.g., glitter, stars, moons)
- ☐ A collection of Asteroid Asks cards
- ☐ A rocket fuel tank (e.g., empty tissue box)
- ☐ Photocopy of rocket fuel tank template for the crew

- [ ] Glue, scissors, tape, colored pencils/markers
- [ ] Mother Ship Update (one copy per Space Traveler). Please give your contact information in the space provided prior to copying

MISSION ITINERARY

Your itinerary for this mission consists of two parts:

Part 1: Preparing to Launch – To Be Completed Before Mission 1 Begins

- [ ] Familiarize yourself with the content of the missions, and in particular Mission 1 (from both your own manual and the Space Traveler manual).
- [ ] Photocopy the Mother Ship Update and equip the mission with the designated mission supplies.
- [ ] Photocopy a sufficient number of Asteroid Ask cards for the duration of the eight-week journey.
- [ ] Prepare the rocket fuel tank.

Part 2: Launching the Mission – Structure for Mission 1

- [ ] Introduce yourself as the Space Guide for the eight-mission journey.
- [ ] Welcome the Space Travelers.
- [ ] Referring to the constellation chart, introduce the purpose of the overall mission and explain the itinerary.
- [ ] Explain the format for each mission (i.e., routine).
- [ ] Hand out a copy of the Space Traveler manual to each participant and have them write their name on their copy. Collect at the end of the session.
- [ ] Have the Space Travelers complete the Space Traveler contract.
- [ ] Have the Space Travelers complete the Space Walk 1 activity.
- [ ] Have the Space Travelers complete the Space Disk activity.
- [ ] Invite the Space Travelers to draw/write/dictate an Asteroid Ask.
- [ ] Answer the Asteroid Asks before the Space Travelers begin work on their space journal.
- [ ] Have the Space Travelers write/draw/dictate in their journal.
- [ ] Hand out a Mother Ship Update for the Space Travelers to take home.
- [ ] Complete the Space Guide's journal.

MISSION 1 ACTIVITIES

Constellation Chart
A visual chart of the eight missions allowing the Space Travelers to plot their space journey. Referring to the constellation chart, identify and introduce the current mission, explain the purpose of the mission and outline the itinerary. The Space Travelers decorate the current mission on their constellation chart.

Space Traveler Contract
A contract for the Space Travelers to complete about the rules they are to follow during each mission (e.g., take turns talking, use kind words, keep hands and objects to self).

Space Walk 1
Relaxation activity that explains to the Space Travelers via visualization the purpose of the space journey.

Space Disk
A self-reflection activity. The Space Travelers complete their own Space Disk to identify personal strengths, interests and abilities.

Asteroid Asks
A question-and-answer clarification activity. The Space Travelers are invited to write/draw/dictate a question on the Asteroid Ask card related to the current mission, whether a question about the mission overview, mission itinerary, and so on. Once completed, the Asteroid Asks are placed in the rocket fuel tank. The Space Guide responds to the Asteroid Asks before the Space Travelers begin to work on their space journals.

Rocket Fuel Tank
A template to be used to cover a rectangular cardboard box (e.g., tissue box) where the Space Travelers place the Asteroid Asks.

Space Journals
A journal that Space Travelers can write/draw/dictate in about what they learned during Mission 1.

Mother Ship Update
A newsletter for home explaining the goals and activities for Mission 1.

Space Guide Journal
A journal for the Space Guide to complete, identifying what went well with the mission, what was problematic, what was unexpected, what would be done differently if the mission was taught again, what questions came up and whether the intended outcomes were achieved.

SPACE TRAVELER CONTRACT

It is important that you as the Space Guide, in conjunction with the Space Travelers, specify the non-negotiable rules that will be followed during the eight-week space journey. Once the rules are specified, ensure that the Space Travelers have a clear understanding of what each rule looks and sounds like. This will involve discussing the purpose of the rules, the definition of what each rule looks and sounds like, as well as role-playing the rule. You may find throughout the eight-week mission that you need to reteach the rules and act in the role of behavior coach with the Space Travelers. Have each Space Traveler complete the contract in his or her manual.

SPACE TRAVELER CONTRACT

We will be talking about peaceful and positive ways to work and play together during our space journey. We have agreed to the following crew rules:

Crew rule 1: _____

Crew rule 2: _____

Crew rule 3: _____

Crew rule 4: _____

Some things I can do that will help me follow our rules:

_____

_____

_____

Do I need help following our rules? (Circle one)   YES   NO
If YES,
       What help do I need?
       Who and when will I ask for help?

_____

I, _____, AGREE to do everything I can to follow our crew rules for the space journey.

Signed

_____   _____
Space Traveler   Space Guide

Date _____

SPACE WALK 1

This is a relaxation, visualization activity where you as Space Guide read the following visualization script to the Space Travelers. The script details the purpose of the eight-week space journey. Explain to the Space Travelers what a visualization is: creating a mental picture of the words being spoken/scene being described, imagining in your mind the scene being described/script being read.

Once the Space Travelers have participated in the Space Walk 1 visualization, invite them to draw their visualization and to share their drawing with two other Space Travelers. Provide prompts if required.

SPACE WALK 1 Script:

You are an astronaut about to embark on a space walk outside of your spacecraft. To participate in this mission you must first reach a completely relaxed state so your body can slip into the specially fitted space suit you are going to wear. You are standing in the airlock of the spacecraft. (Pause)

Close your eyes. (Pause) To reach this super-relaxed state, you must focus on your breathing. Don't change your breathing. (Pause) Just listen to your breath and breathe in and out as you would normally do. (Pause) As you breathe out, say to yourself the word "relax." Breathe in, then breathe out saying the word "relax" to yourself again. (Allow a minute for the Space Travelers to practice.)

You are now ready to be placed into your space suit. The Space Engineer* helps you into your suit. Once you are fitted into your space suit and helmet, the Space Engineer seals the hatch behind you. You are not alone in the airlock. The other Space Travelers and your Space Engineer are with you. (Pause) You can hear a hissing noise as the air is being pumped out of the airlock. (Pause) Now we will start a countdown from 10 to 1. (Pause) When we reach number 1, you will be in a super-relaxed state in your space suit and be ready to space walk.

10. You feel your whole body starting to melt into the space suit. (Pause)
9. You feel your body sinking into the suit's various compartments. (Pause)
8. You feel your eyes, mouth and face relax. (Pause)
7. You feel your neck muscles relax. (Pause)
6. You feel your arms become heavy. (Pause)
5. You feel your stomach relax. (Pause)
4. You feel your legs turn jelly-like. (Pause)
3. You feel your feet relax. (Pause)
2. You are in a completely relaxed state. (Pause)
1. You are in a super-relaxed and calm state. (Pause)

*The person who takes the children on their space walk. This could be an OT/PT, an aide or anybody else with the prerequisite skills.

MISSION 1

Your body is limp and like jelly. (Pause) Now your body is a perfect fit with your space suit and you are ready to exit the airlock. A hatch slides open and the Space Engineer steps into space. One by one, you also step out and join up. (Pause) You are floating, but you are attached to your spacecraft with a safety line. (Pause) You can see your fellow Space Travelers with their space suits and helmets on. (Pause) You can see the stars and the planets. You can see earth. (Pause) A friendly alien hovers in his spacecraft close-by. His job is to share with you what you are going to be learning during this mission. Listen carefully to what he has to say. (Pause – Space Engineer, please modulate your voice to take on the character of the alien.)

> Greetings. My name is Neila. I come from the planet ECAEP, where peace and positive thinking has been our way of life for the past 20 billion years. We have learned how important it is to work and play together in a peaceful and positive way. I have been chosen to share my planet's wisdom with your Space Guide about living in this way.
>
> You will be traveling together on eight missions, where you will learn about feelings, thinking, staying calm and solving problems with your crew. We have given this mission a space theme. You may have thought you were learning about space, but you will be learning about working and playing together in a peaceful and positive way. (Pause)
>
> I will now share this wisdom with your Space Engineer. We will leave you for a few minutes while you and the other Space Travelers can have some fun. Imagine that you are floating together in space doing somersaults and cartwheels. (Pause) I know you will learn important things in your space journey.

Now it is time to go back into your spacecraft. (Pause) Wave goodbye to Neila. (Pause) Have a last look around at the stars, planets and earth. (Pause) The hatch opens. (Pause) You all step into the airlock. (Pause) The hatch closes behind you. The air is pumped back into the airlock. (Pause) You remove your helmets. The Space Engineer helps you out of your suits. (Pause) You are now ready to come back into the space ship.

Open your eyes and wriggle your fingers and toes.
Welcome back!

Drawing Prompts for Visualization Activity:

If necessary, you may help the Space Travelers get started with their drawings using the following prompts:

- You as an astronaut

- Your spacecraft

- Your specially fitted space suit

- Wearing your space suit and helmet

- Standing in the airlock of the spacecraft

- Exiting the airlock

- Going on your space walk

- Floating in space attached to the spacecraft with a safety line

- Your fellow Space Travelers with their space suits and helmets on

- The stars, the planets

- Earth

- A friendly alien, Neila

- The message Neila shared with you about the mission

- The planet ECAEP

- Entering the spacecraft

- Coming back into the space ship

SPACE DISK

This is a self-reflection activity where Space Travelers take a little time to think about themselves – their strengths, abilities, worries, etc. Following a written format – known as a Space Disk – Space Travelers record/dictate their responses to 10 questions about themselves. When all the questions on the Space Disk have been answered, the Space Guide invites the Space Travelers to share two sections of their Space Disk with another Space Traveler.

Here is one way of introducing this activity to the Space Travelers.

Hi, just like I have different programs inside my spacecraft computer, you also have many different characteristics inside of you. Let us log onto this game by inputting your name in the center of the Space Disk. Now it is your Space Disk. Complete the sentences on each section of the disk. Answers such as "I don't know" or "nothing" will not compute. I like to learn more about your characteristics, just as you like to learn more about space. Ask your Space Guide to help you complete your Space Disk and then share two sections of your Space Disk with another Space Traveler.

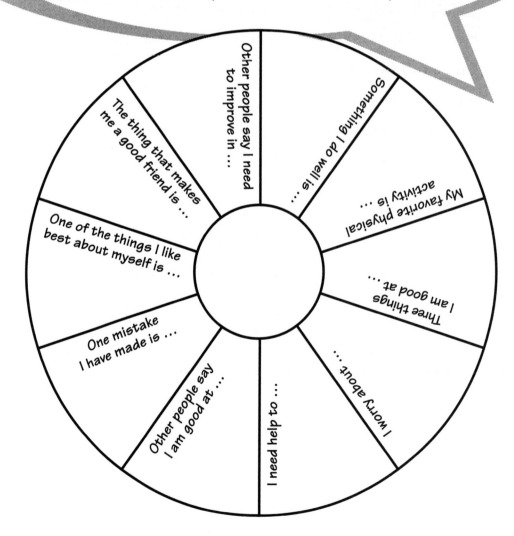

Other people say I need to improve in …

Something I do well is …

The thing that makes me a good friend is …

My favorite physical activity is …

One of the things I like best about myself is …

Three things I am good at …

One mistake I have made is …

I worry about …

Other people say I am good at …

I need help to …

ASTEROID ASKS

The purpose of the Asteroids Asks activity, which is part of each mission, is for the Space Travelers to ask the Space Guide questions about the current mission. In other words, it is a question-and-answer clarification activity that takes place after the core activities have been completed. The Space Travelers are invited to write/draw/dictate a question on the Asteroid Ask card related to the mission. Once they have completed their Asteroid Asks, the Space Travelers place them in the rocket fuel tank. Space Travelers do not have to complete Asteroid Asks. It is a voluntary activity.

Your role as Space Guide is to respond to each Asteroid Asks card before the Space Travelers work on their space journal. You may choose to respond to the Asteroid Asks on your own or invite assistance/ideas from the crew.

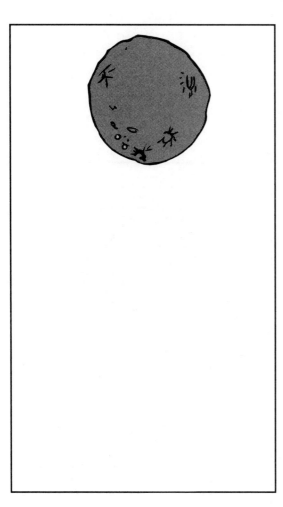

From Carter, M., & Santomauro, J. (2004). *Space travelers.* Shawnee Mission, KS: Autism Asperger Publishing Company. Copied with permission.

MISSION 1

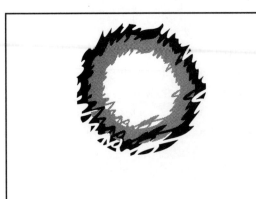

ROCKET FUEL TANK

The Rocket Fuel Tank is a template to be photocopied and used to cover a rectangular cardboard box (e.g., empty tissue box) where the

written/drawn Asteroid Asks are placed. If you are working with an entire class, you may find that you need a large rocket fuel tank. When working with a small group of Space Travelers, a small rocket fuel tank is appropriate.

Your role as Space Guide is to provide the rocket fuel tank material and equipment, assign group roles, check for understanding, monitor while the group works and intervene if and when necessary. Group roles may include:

- **Material and Equipment Manager:** Collects and distributes material and equipment needed to construct the rocket fuel tank
- **Listener:** Repeats and clarifies the task that has been assigned
- **Questioner:** Seeks information from all group members
- **Timekeeper:** Monitors time and reminds group of time
- **Cutter:** Cuts material and equipment as agreed
- **Gluer:** Glues material and equipment as agreed
- **Ideas Manager:** Comes with up ideas for how to use material and equipment
- **Encourager:** Supports all group members
- **Scout:** Gets relevant information from Space Guide when necessary

If you choose to introduce group roles, make sure that you have a clear description of each role to avoid confusion and frustration among crew members. Once each role description has been discussed with the group, create a visual prompt card for each role using the suggestions above. This can act as a prompt, not only for the role holder but for all group members. You can either assign roles or invite Space Travelers to select a role that they would like to perform.

As Space Guide, invite all the Space Travelers to decorate the crew's rocket fuel tank.

ROCKET FUEL TANK

MOTHER SHIP UPDATE

The purpose of the Mother Ship Update is to share what is happening during the Space Travelers' missions. This way parents/guardians know the goals and outcomes of each mission, making them better able to discuss with their children what activities they engaged in during each mission, what they learned, what they enjoyed, and so on.

At the conclusion of each mission, give each Space Traveler a Mother Ship Update to take home. It is the Space Travelers' responsibility to take the update home. It is the joint responsibility of the Space Traveler and the Mother Ship (parent/guardian) to share the update with one another.

MOTHER SHIP UPDATE

Hello Parents/Guardians,

This is your first Mother Ship Update. If you have any questions, please do not hesitate to contact me. My contact information is as follows:

Name: _____

Phone: _____

Fax: _____

E-mail: _____

Constellation Chart

MISSION 1

LAUNCH PAD

MISSION 5

ATMOSPHERIC PRESSURE

MISSION 2

INTRODUCING THE CREW

MISSION 6

MISSION CONTROL

MISSION 3

STARLIGHT AND GRAVITY THINKING

MISSION 7

SPACE WALKING – PREPARING FOR LANDING

MISSION 4

THE FEELINGS SHUTTLE

MISSION 8

TOUCHDOWN PARTY

MISSION 1

The goals for Mission 1 were to introduce and familiarize the Space Travelers with the purpose of the eight-week space journey, the constellation chart, their role in the overall mission and tasks specific to Mission 1.

This is the foundation mission, preparing the team with the equipment they will require for the whole journey.

The Space Travelers were introduced and asked to commit themselves to the space contract – the team rules they are to follow during each mission.

MISSION OUTCOMES
Students:

* Learned the purpose of the *Space Travelers* journey

* Became familiar with the eight-week *Space Travelers* journey

28

SPACE TRAVELER'S JOURNAL

The Space Traveler's journal is completed by the Space Travelers at the end of each mission. Sentence starters are provided to assist them with their reflective thinking. Space Travelers can write/draw or dictate their thoughts in response to each sentence starter.

SPACE TRAVELER'S JOURNAL

Date: _____

What I liked about today's mission:

New ideas I have learned:

What interested me most:

I'm curious about:

Actions I'm going to take:

MISSION 1

SPACE GUIDE'S JOURNAL

This journal is completed by the Space Guide at the end of each mission to identify what went well with the mission, what was problematic, what was unexpected, what would be done differently if the mission was taught again, what questions came up during the mission, and so on.

Date: _____

What went well:

What was problematic:

What was unexpected:

What I would do differently if I taught this mission again:

What questions were raised for me during this mission:

Additional comments:

INTRODUCING THE CREW
SPACE GUIDE'S MAINTENANCE CHECKLIST

MISSION AHEAD

Your goal as Space Guide for Mission 2 is to assist the Space Travelers in recognizing and communicating their own and others' individual strengths, abilities and interests.

MISSION OUTCOMES

Space Travelers will:

☐ Recognize and communicate their own and others' individual strengths, abilities and interests

☐ Learn a little more about their own and others' individual strengths, abilities and interests

☐ Promote effective communication, including listening to understand and speaking to be understood

MISSION LENGTH

1-1/2 hrs.

MISSION SUPPLIES

You will need the following:

☐ Space Traveler manual (one copy per Space Traveler)

☐ A collection of Asteroid Asks cards

☐ A rocket fuel tank

☐ Photocopies of Space Charade cards cut out

☐ A roll of paper (Space Suit activity)

☐ Scissors, colored pencils/markers (Space Suit activity)

☐ Mother Ship Update (one copy per Space Traveler). Please give your contact information in the space provided prior to copying

MISSION ITINERARY

Your itinerary for this mission is in two parts:

Part 1: Preparing to Launch – To Be Completed Before Mission 2 Begins

☐ Familiarize yourself with the content of Mission 2 (both from your manual and the Space Traveler manual).

☐ Photocopy Space Charade cards and cut them out.

☐ Prepare items for the Space Suit activity.

☐ Photocopy Mother Ship Update.

☐ Provide blank Asteroid Ask cards.

Part 2: Launching Mission – Structure for Mission 2

☐ Welcome the Space Travelers.

☐ Referring to the constellation chart, introduce the overall purpose of the mission and explain the itinerary.

☐ Hand out the Space Traveler manuals and collect at the end of the session.

☐ Revisit and reteach the rules agreed to in the space contract.

☐ Have the Space Travelers do the Space Log activity.

☐ Have the Space Travelers complete the Space Charades activity.

☐ Have the Space Travelers complete the Star Qualities activity.

☐ Have the Space Travelers complete the Space Suit activity.

☐ Invite the Space Travelers to draw/write/dictate an Asteroid Ask.

☐ Answer the Asteroid Asks before the Space Travelers begin work on their space journal.

☐ Have the Space Travelers write/draw/dictate in their space journal.

☐ Hand out a Mother Ship Update for Space Travelers to take home.

☐ Complete the Space Guide's journal.

MISSION 2 ACTIVITIES

Constellation Chart
A visual chart of the eight missions allowing the Space Travelers to plot their space journey. (Space Travelers decorate current mission.)

Space Traveler Contract
Rules agreed to in the space contract. (Revisit and reteach as needed.)

Space Log
An interview activity where the Space Travelers interview each other in pairs to gain knowledge of their view of themselves. Once they have completed the log, each pair shares their interview information with another pair.

Space Charades
A role-play activity where the Space Travelers mime their answers to the question on the Space Charades card, identifying personal responses to social scenarios.

Star Qualities
A verbal/written activity where the Space Travelers give compliments to themselves and to other crew members.

Space Suit
A cooperative activity where the Space Travelers design their own space suit.

Asteroid Asks
A question-and-answer clarification activity. The Space Travelers are invited to write/draw/dictate a question on the Asteroid Ask card related to the current mission, whether a question about the mission overview, mission itinerary, and so on. Once completed, the Asteroid Asks are placed in the rocket fuel tank. The Space Guide responds to the Asteroid Asks before the Space Travelers begin to work on their space journals.

Space Journals
A journal that Space Travelers can write/draw/dictate in about what they learned during Mission 2.

Mother Ship Update
A newsletter for home explaining the goals and activities for Mission 2.

Space Guide Journal
A journal for the Space Guide to complete, identifying what went well with the mission, what was problematic, what was unexpected, what would be done differently if the mission was taught again, what questions came up and whether the intended outcomes were achieved.

MISSION 2

SPACE LOG

This is an interview activity where the Space Travelers work in pairs interviewing one another to determine their view on different aspects of themselves. Once interviews are completed, each pair joins with another pair and shares the information gathered during the interview.

The purpose of this activity is to help the Space Travelers get to know themselves better, and to get to know their fellow Space Travelers a little more as well.

Interview Questions

My Own Point of View

🎧 LISTENER_____   🎤 SPEAKER_____

🎧 What are some interesting things about you?

🎤 _____

🎧 Name three things you like to do with other people.

🎤   1. _____

    2. _____

    3. _____

🎧 If you could go on a trip, where would you go? Who would you go with?

🎤 _____

🎧 What is something you think about a lot?

🎤 _____

🎧 What do you like best about being you?

🎤 _____

SPACE LOG cont.

🎧 Tell me about a time when you had a lot of fun.

🎤 _____

🎧 What would you do if you didn't have to go to school all day?

🎤 _____

🎧 Tell me about a time when you did something even though you were feeling very nervous about doing it.

🎤 _____

🎧 Tell me about a time when you did something that helped someone else.

🎤 _____

🎧 Tell me about a time when you kept trying at something and didn't give up, even though it was hard to do.

🎤 _____

🎧 Is there something you'd like to tell me about yourself that I haven't already asked you?

🎤 _____

SPACE CHARADES

The Space Travelers select a Space Charade card from the deck of cards and take turns thinking about their personal response to the question on the card. Then they write/draw their responses below the questions on the Space Charades cards on the worksheet in their manual. Once this has been done, invite the Space Travelers to take turns miming their response to the questions to the crew.

The audience/remaining crew members guess what the Space Traveler is communicating through the mime. Space Travelers can give as little or as much information as they choose in their mime.

The object of the game is for the Space Travelers who are miming their response to the Space Charade cards to share something about themselves with crew members in a fun and nonthreatening way. The crew takes turns guessing what the mime means, and when they work it out, they learn a little more about their fellow Space Traveler. The Space Traveler who guesses the correct answer first gets the next turn.

The Space Guide's role is to facilitate the game, be the time keeper and ensure that the game is played fairly and cooperatively. This game can be played in small groups or with the whole crew.

Before the game begins, you will need to photocopy the cards on the following page and cut them out. You can add other cards with different questions written on them.

MISSION 2

What is your
favorite song?

What is
your favorite
TV show?

What is your
favorite food?

How many
brothers and
sisters do
you have?

What physical
activity
do you like
to do?

What is your
favorite hobby?

What do you
like to do
after school?

What is your
middle name?

STAR QUALITIES

This is a verbal/written activity where the Space Travelers give themselves two compliments in conjunction with also giving other crew members two compliments. The purpose of the activity is to teach giving and receiving compliments.

As Space Guide you may give some examples of compliments or some sentence starters for Space Travelers to use, such as the following.

Sample Compliments:

☘ "I like the fact that I am great at catching whenever we play baseball."

☘ "I am an interesting painter as I mix lots of different colors and textures together."

☘ "I am very persistent when it comes to fixing problems on the computer."

☘ "I like the way you always ask if you can help."

☘ "I think you are a very caring friend."

Sample Sentence Starters:

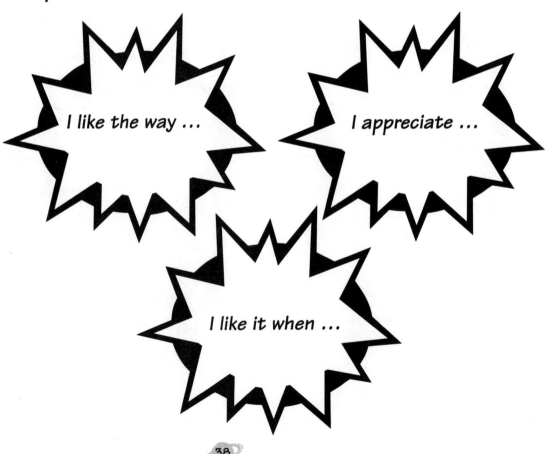

I like the way ...

I appreciate ...

I like it when ...

Sample Sentence Starters (cont.):

I think you ...

Something I do well is ...

I think I am ...

You always ...

People like me because ...

I especially like the way ...

SPACE SUIT

This is a cooperative activity where the Space Travelers trace the outline of each other's bodies. This outline forms the template of their space suit. Space Travelers decorate their space suits before they are displayed in the classroom. The decorations chosen by the Space Travelers are to reflect their personal identity – who they are, what they think is important, what they stand for, what qualities they have, their interests, strengths, and so on.

MOTHER SHIP UPDATE

MISSION 2

Hello Parents/Guardians,

This is your second Mother Ship Update. If you have any questions, please do not hesitate to contact me. My contact information is as follows:

Name: _____

Phone: _____

Fax: _____

E-mail: _____

MISSION 2

The goal for Mission 2 was to assist the Space Travelers in recognizing and communicating their own and others' strengths, abilities and interests.

MISSION OUTCOMES

Students:

- 🌏 Recognized and communicated their own and others' strengths, abilities and interests

- 🌏 Learned more about their own and others' individual strengths, abilities and interests

- 🌏 Promoted effective communication, including listening to understand and speaking to be understood

Constellation Chart

MISSION 1
LAUNCH PAD

MISSION 5
ATMOSPHERIC PRESSURE

MISSION 2
INTRODUCING THE CREW

MISSION 6
MISSION CONTROL

MISSION 3
STARLIGHT AND GRAVITY THINKING

MISSION 7
SPACE WALKING – PREPARING FOR LANDING

MISSION 4
THE FEELINGS SHUTTLE

MISSION 8
TOUCHDOWN PARTY

SPACE TRAVELER'S JOURNAL

Date: _____

What I liked about today's mission:

New ideas I have learned:

What interested me most:

I'm curious about:

Actions I'm going to take:

SPACE GUIDE'S JOURNAL

This journal is completed by the Space Guide at the end of each mission to identify what went well with the mission, what was problematic, what was unexpected, what would be done differently if the mission was taught again, what questions came up during the mission, and so on.

Date: _____

What went well:

What was problematic:

What was unexpected:

What I would do differently if I taught this mission again:

What questions were raised for me during this mission:

Additional comments:

STARLIGHT AND GRAVITY THINKING

SPACE GUIDE'S MAINTENANCE CHECKLIST

MISSION AHEAD
Your goals as Space Guide for Mission 3 is to assist the Space Travelers in learning more about helpful (positive) and unhelpful (negative) ways of thinking.

MISSION OUTCOMES
Space Travelers will:

- ☐ Explore the connection between thinking, feeling and doing
- ☐ Differentiate between positive and negative thinking
- ☐ Begin/continue learning about the importance of thinking in a positive way

MISSION LENGTH
1-1/2 hrs.

MISSION SUPPLIES
You will need the following:

- ☐ Space Traveler manual (a copy per Space Traveler)
- ☐ A collection of Asteroid Asks
- ☐ A rocket fuel tank
- ☐ Samples of coats of arms for display – Space Shield activity
- ☐ Photocopies of Alien Acts cards x 2 (= 12 cards)
- ☐ Colored pencils/markers
- ☐ Mother Ship Update (a copy per Space Traveler). Please give your contact information in the space provided prior to copying

MISSION 3

MISSION ITINERARY
Your itinerary for this mission is in two parts:

Part 1: Preparing to Launch – To Be Completed Before Mission 3 Begins

☐ Familiarize yourself with the content of Mission 3 (both from your manual and the Space Traveler manual).

☐ Photocopy Alien Acts cards x 2 (= 12 cards) and cut out.

☐ Photocopy Mother Ship Update.

☐ Provide blank Asteroid Ask cards.

Part 2: Launching Mission – Structure for Mission 3

☐ Welcome the Space Travelers.

☐ Referring to the constellation chart, introduce the purpose of the overall mission and explain the itinerary.

☐ Hand out the Space Traveler manuals and collect at the end of the session.

☐ Revisit and reteach the rules agreed to in the space contract.

☐ Have the Space Travelers complete the Adventures of the Starlights and the Gravities activity.

☐ Have the Space Travelers complete the Cartoon Clusters activity.

☐ Have the Space Travelers complete the Space Shield activity.

☐ Have the Space Travelers complete the Alien Acts activity.

☐ Invite the Space Travelers to draw/write/dictate an Asteroid Ask.

☐ Answer the Asteroid Asks before the Space Travelers begin working on their space journal.

☐ Have the Space Travelers write/draw/dictate in their space journal.

☐ Hand out a Mother Ship Update to the Space Travelers to take home.

☐ Complete the Space Guide's journal.

MISSION 3 ACTIVITIES

Constellation Chart
A visual chart of the eight missions allowing the Space Travelers to plot their space journey. (Space Travelers decorate current mission.)

Space Traveler Contract
Rules agreed to in the space contract. (Revisit and reteach as needed.)

The Adventures of the Starlights and the Gravities
A creative writing activity where the Space Travelers receive a scenario and are invited to formulate two different stories based on the same scenario. The purpose of this activity is to help the Space Travelers gain insight into positive and negative ways of thinking about the same situation.

Cartoon Clusters
A graphic art activity where the Space Travelers design their own cartoons using the characters from the Starlight and Gravity families, identifying positive and negative ways of thinking about the same situation.

Space Shield
A design activity where the Space Travelers create two family shields:
• Starlight family
• Gravity family

Alien Acts
A role-play activity where the Space Travelers respond to social scenarios outlined on cards using either positive or negative thinking.

Asteroid Asks
A question-and-answer clarification activity. The Space Travelers are invited to write/draw/dictate a question on the Asteroid Ask card related to the current mission, whether a question about the mission overview, mission itinerary, and so on. Once completed, the Asteroid Asks are placed in the rocket fuel tank. The Space Guide responds to the Asteroid Asks before the Space Travelers begin to work on their space journals.

Space Journals
A journal that Space Travelers can write/draw/dictate in about what they learned during Mission 3.

Mother Ship Update
A newsletter for home explaining the goals and activities for Mission 3.

Space Guide Journal
A journal for the Space Guide to complete, identifying what went well with the mission, what was problematic, what was unexpected, what would be done differently if the mission was taught again, what questions came up and whether the intended outcomes were achieved.

THE ADVENTURES OF THE STARLIGHTS AND THE GRAVITIES

Introduce the Space Travelers to the concept of positive and negative thinking by telling a story that involves the Starlight and the Gravity families. In the story both families experience the same situation, but think about it very differently. The Starlights think about the situation from a positive, optimistic perspective whereas the Gravities think about it from a negative, pessimistic perspective. Consequently, the Starlights and the Gravities experience different feelings and emotions based on and associated with their thinking. This in turn influences what they do and say – how they behave.

Scenarios:

Meet the Starlights and the Gravities. The Starlight family looks on the bright side of things, whereas the Gravities always look on the gloomy side of things.

🌑 The Gravity family has a habit of thinking in negative ways about everything. Therefore, you hear them saying things like "It's not fair!" "This is awful." "I should have …" "I'm a loser." Their way of thinking is unhelpful as it often leads them to feel down and then to make unhelpful choices about situations.

🌑 The Starlight family thinks differently about situations. They might think something is disappointing, upsetting, annoying, and so on, but they do not think it is all completely negative. They try to see the good side of a situation. You often hear them saying, "I know it's hard, but I'll keep trying." "I'm smart and I can do it!" Their thinking is helpful, which leads them to feel more positive about situations and to act in a more positive and constructive manner.

Ask the Space Travelers to:

1. Listen to each story starter and think about the Starlights' and the Gravities' approach to situations.

2. Write, type or dictate a short story about the adventures of the two families.

3. Compare and contrast stories with those of the other Space Travelers.

ADVENTURES cont.

Starlight Scenario:

_____

_____

_____

_____

_____

_____

_____

Gravity Scenario:

_____

_____

_____

_____

_____

_____

_____

CARTOON CLUSTERS

In this graphic art activity, the Space Travelers design their own cartoon using characters from the Starlight and Gravity families. It is an extension of "The Adventures of the Starlights and the Gravities." The Space Travelers are now asked to visually depict family members of the Starlight and Gravity families interacting with one another in an exciting adventure. Emphasize that the Space Travelers have to use talking and thinking bubbles to illustrate the different thinking approaches of the various family members:

STARLIGHT family – positive ways of thinking about the situation (e.g., This is disappointing/I will give it a try/I can do this/Sometimes this happens).

GRAVITY family – negative ways of thinking of the situation (e.g., This is the worst thing that could happen/This will never work/I can't/It always happens).

Space Travelers work in pairs and design their cartoon using the following characters:

- Sam Starlight
- Gary Gravity
- Sarah Starlight
- Gemma Gravity

Directions:

1. Remember that Sam and Sarah Starlight are members of the Starlight family and, therefore, think in a helpful and positive way. Gary and Gemma, on the other hand, are members of the Gravity family and think in an unhelpful and negative way.

2. Use both talking and thinking bubbles to show what the characters are thinking about and saying to each other.

SPACE SHIELD

In this design activity the Space Travelers work in pairs to create two separate space shields, each communicating very different information:

STARLIGHT family – communicating helpful, positive, optimistic thinking

GRAVITY family – communicating unhelpful, negative, pessimistic thinking

Emphasize to the Space Travelers the importance of each shield depicting different approaches in thinking, feeling and doing. For example, discuss the fact that the Starlights' shield must give a very strong message about how they think about things (e.g., "This is hard, but I will give it a go"). In contrast, the Gravity family's shield must send a very strong message about how the Gravities think about things (e.g., "This is hard. I will never get it right").

Ask the Space Travelers to work with a crew member whom they have not worked with during today's mission.

Before the Space Travelers begin to create their shields, ask them to think about what they plan to include on their shields and to discuss their thoughts with one another. Encourage them to reach an agreement on what to include on their shields. When the shields are finished, display them in the room for the entire crew to see.

STARLIGHT FAMILY SHIELD

GRAVITY FAMILY SHIELD

MISSION 3

ALIEN ACTS

This is a role-play activity where the Space Travelers, working in pairs, respond to a scenario selected from a deck of cards with either Starlight (positive) or Gravity (negative) thinking and act it out in front of the rest of the crew.

Before the game begins, the Space Travelers decide who in the pair will take the role of Starlight thinking and who will take the role of Gravity thinking.

Each team must be original in its thinking. The rest of the crew determines if the role-play represents Starlight or Gravity thinking. Space Travelers must give at least one reason in support of their claim.

As the Space Guide, act as time keeper and Alien Acts creator. Here are some Alien Acts scenarios to begin with.

Alien Acts Cards

You are playing a game with the other Space Travelers and the siren sounds for you to return to your spacecraft.

You receive an unexpected gift from your Space Guide.

The computer crashes with all your space project work on it.

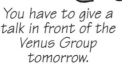

You have to give a talk in front of the Venus Group tomorrow.

You cannot go to space camp because you have planet pox.

Some of the aliens are bullying you.

54

MOTHER SHIP UPDATE

MISSION 3

Hello Parents/Guardians,

This is your third Mother Ship Update. If you have any questions, please do not hesitate to contact me. My contact information is as follows:

Name: _____

Phone: _____

Fax: _____

E-mail: _____

MISSION 3

The goal for Mission 3 was to assist the Space Travelers in learning more about helpful (positive) and unhelpful (negative) ways of thinking.

MISSION OUTCOMES

Students:

- Explored the connection between thinking, feeling and doing

- Differentiated between positive and negative thinking

- Began learning about the importance of thinking in positive ways

Constellation Chart

MISSION 1
LAUNCH PAD

MISSION 5
ATMOSPHERIC PRESSURE

MISSION 2
INTRODUCING THE CREW

MISSION 6
MISSION CONTROL

MISSION 3
STARLIGHT AND GRAVITY THINKING

MISSION 7
SPACE WALKING – PREPARING FOR LANDING

MISSION 4
THE FEELINGS SHUTTLE

MISSION 8
TOUCHDOWN PARTY

SPACE TRAVELER'S JOURNAL

Date: _____

What I liked about today's mission:

New ideas I have learned:

What interested me most:

I'm curious about:

Actions I'm going to take:

SPACE GUIDE'S JOURNAL

This journal is completed by the Space Guide at the end of each mission to identify what went well with the mission, what was problematic, what was unexpected, what would be done differently if the mission was taught again, what questions came up during the mission, and so on.

Date: _____

What went well:

What was problematic:

What was unexpected:

What I would do differently if I taught this mission again:

What questions were raised for me during this mission:

Additional comments:

THE FEELINGS SHUTTLE

SPACE GUIDE'S MAINTENANCE CHECKLIST

MISSION AHEAD

Your goals as Space Guide for Mission 4 is to assist the Space Travelers in learning more about their own and other people's emotions.

MISSION OUTCOMES

Space Travelers will:

- ☐ Expand their emotions vocabulary
- ☐ Become aware that everyone has emotions unique to him/herself
- ☐ Deepen their understanding of different emotions

MISSION LENGTH

1-1/2 hrs.

MISSION SUPPLIES

You will need the following:

- ☐ Space Traveler manual (a copy per Space Traveler)
- ☐ A collection of Asteroid Asks
- ☐ A rocket fuel tank
- ☐ Dictionary
- ☐ Photocopies of Suspended Stars activity (one per Space Traveler)
- ☐ Scissors, colored pencils/markers, hole punch, string/yarn
- ☐ Mother Ship Update (one copy per Space Traveler). Please give your contact information in the space provided prior to copying

MISSION 4

MISSION ITINERARY
Your itinerary for this mission is in two parts:

Part 1: Preparing to Launch – To Be Completed Before Mission 4 Begins

☐ Familiarize yourself with the content of Mission 4 (both from your manual and the Space Traveler manual).

☐ Photocopy the Suspended Stars (one per Space Traveler).

☐ Photocopy the Mother Ship Update.

☐ Provide blank Asteroid Ask cards.

Part 2: Launching Mission – Structure for Mission 4

☐ Welcome the Space Travelers.

☐ Referring to the constellation chart, introduce the purpose of the overall mission and explain the itinerary.

☐ Hand out the Space Traveler manuals and collect at the end of the session.

☐ Revisit and reteach the rules agreed to in the space contract.

☐ Have the Space Travelers complete the Telescopic Word Search activity.

☐ Have the Space Travelers complete the First Contact activity.

☐ Have the Space Travelers complete the Suspended Stars activity.

☐ Have the Space Travelers complete the Alien Features activity.

☐ Invite the Space Travelers to draw/write/dictate an Asteroid Ask.

☐ Answer the Asteroid Asks before the Space Travelers start working on their space journal.

☐ Have the Space Travelers write/draw/dictate in their space journal.

☐ Hand out a Mother Ship Update to the Space Traveler to take home.

☐ Complete the Space Guide's journal.

MISSION 4 ACTIVITIES

Constellation Chart
A visual chart of the eight missions allowing the Space Travelers to plot their space journey. (Space Travelers decorate current mission.)

Space Traveler Contract
Rules agreed to in the space contract. (Revisit and reteach as needed.)

Telescopic Word Search
An emotions word search where the Space Travelers complete the word search, discuss emotions and act them out to further expand their emotions vocabulary.

First Contact
A writing/illustrating activity in which the Space Travelers write and draw responses to social scenarios specific to a given emotion.

Suspended Stars
A craft activity where the Space Travelers design their own mobile reflecting specific emotions to deepen their understanding of emotions.

Alien Features
A drawing activity where the Space Travelers depict specific facial expressions that reflect different emotions.

Asteroid Asks
A question-and-answer clarification activity. The Space Travelers are invited to write/draw/dictate a question on the Asteroid Ask card related to the current mission, whether a question about the mission overview, mission itinerary, and so on. Once completed, the Asteroid Asks are placed in the rocket fuel tank. The Space Guide responds to the Asteroid Asks before the Space Travelers begin to work on their space journals.

Space Journals
A journal that Space Travelers can write/draw/dictate in about what they learned during Mission 4.

Mother Ship Update
A newsletter for home explaining the goals and activities for Mission 4.

Space Guide Journal
A journal for the Space Guide to complete, identifying what went well with the mission, what was problematic, what was unexpected, what would be done differently if the mission was taught again, what questions came up and whether the intended outcomes were achieved.

TELESCOPIC WORD SEARCH

In this activity you as the Space Guide work with the Space Travelers to (a) extend their emotions vocabulary, (b) expand their understanding of different emotions, and (c) make connections between body signals and emotions.

After completing the emotions word search, discuss with the Space Travelers the meaning of the emotions named in the word search. It is also useful to give and/or solicit practical examples of when Space Travelers have experienced particular emotions – either real or fantasy. Ask the Space Travelers to demonstrate with their bodies how they portray particular emotions. It may be useful to provide a scenario in which an emotion is experienced. This will create a context.

This activity is divided into three parts:

🜨 The Space Travelers work with a partner to complete the emotions word search.

🜨 The Space Travelers work together as a crew to discuss the meaning of each emotion in the list.

🜨 The Space Travelers give an example of a time when they experienced the emotion. Have them take turns showing how their body would respond to each of the emotions.

TELESCOPIC WORD SEARCH cont.

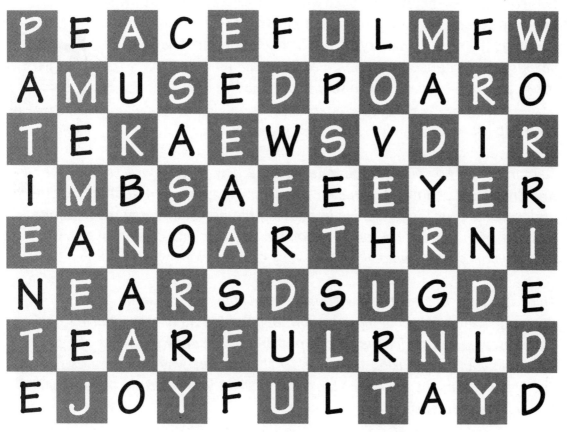

First find and circle the words below. Put the remaining letters together to make a word that names an emotion that everybody feels sometimes.

Clues: You might feel a bit awkward or bashful.

MAD	FRIENDLY	PEACEFUL
ANGRY	AMUSED	WEAK
UPSET	WORRIED	PATIENT
HURT	TENSE	SAD
LOVE	SAFE	TEARFUL
JOYFUL	SORRY	

(Did you know that everybody thinks, feels and acts in different ways in response to the same emotions?)

Answer : EMBARRASSED

FIRST CONTACT

Talk with the Space Travelers about how helpful it can be to put yourself in someone else's shoes – in other words, seeing the situation the way another person sees it, also called *perspective taking*. Point out that it is helpful to try to see things from another's perspective because it gives you an idea about why the other person is behaving the way he or she is.

Example:

Samuh is new to your school. In fact, he is new to the town, the state, and the whole country. He speaks another language and does not understand your language. He is missing his homeland very much, along with his friends from his last school, his teacher and classmates. At playtime he sits by himself looking very sad and lonely.

Think for a minute about how tough everything is for Samuh at the moment. Rather than using put-downs, laughing at him or ignoring him, you may be a little friendlier, more patient and more welcoming of Samuh joining in your play. Taking the time to think about why Samuh is behaving the way he is might help you think about what you could do to help him feel a little less sad and lonely.

Involve the Space Travelers in conversations about social situations that can be viewed differently depending on participants' thinking and feelings.

Working on their own, the Space Travelers:

1. Read and think about the scenarios presented on the worksheet

2. Draw a picture about the characters in each scenario, using thinking and talking bubbles

3. Write about a time when they themselves experienced a similar emotion as the character in the scenario

Once the Space Travelers have written their stories, invite each of them to share his or her experience/s with the crew.

Tauri is happy and excited because it is his birthday tomorrow.

Imagine you are Tauri and draw a picture of how he is feeling.

What is something you feel or felt happy and excited about?

Marsden is angry when her friend Eclipse says she cannot play space ball.

Imagine you are Marsden and draw a picture of how she is feeling.

What do you do when you are feeling or have felt angry?

Nadir is sad when her close friend Aquila tells her that her family is moving away to another planet and she has to change space school.

Imagine you are Nadir saying goodbye to Aquila and draw a picture of the scene.

What is something you feel or felt sad about?

Jasper is feeling courageous when he has a turn on the spiral galaxy ride.

Imagine you are Jasper and draw a picture of him having a turn on the spiral galaxy ride.

Write about a time when you were courageous.

MISSION 4

SUSPENDED STARS

Introduce and explain the sequence of this activity to the Space Travelers and then act as a coach throughout the activity. Rather than answering the questions for the Space Travelers, engage them in conversations, guiding them to find the answers for themselves. It is important that the Space Travelers are not writing words for the sake of writing words, but that they have a clear understanding of what each word means. This is where your role as Space Guide is important. Monitor and track each Space Traveler's understanding of the concepts in the mobile, providing clarification, support and extension as appropriate.

Directions:

Working in pairs, the Space Travelers select an emotion for their suspended star mobile. They answer the sequence of questions on the suspended stars cards using a dictionary, if appropriate/necessary. Finally, they decorate the cards, hole punch and thread them together to create a mobile, which is hung in the classroom.

Before the Space Travelers begin the activity, demonstrate each stage of the activity:

1. Name of emotion: WORRIED

2. Describe the emotion: CONCERNED ABOUT WHAT MIGHT HAPPEN

3. Other words to describe this emotion: ANXIOUS, AFRAID, FEARFUL

4. Opposite emotion: CALM, UNAFRAID, FEARLESS

5. Draw a picture of someone feeling this emotion

MISSION 4

(1)
Name of emotion

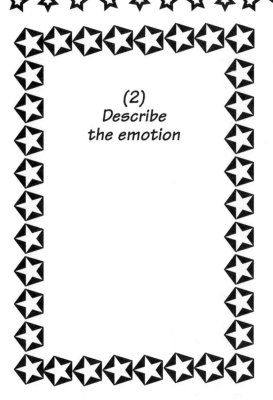

(2)
Describe
the emotion

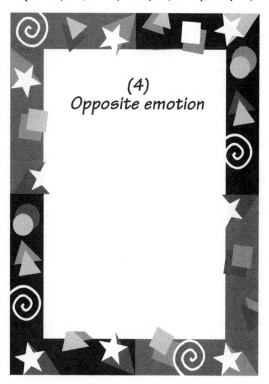

(4)
Opposite emotion

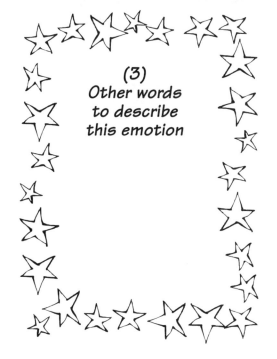

(3)
Other words
to describe
this emotion

(5)
Draw a picture
of someone feeling
this emotion

67

ALIEN FEATURES

It is important that the Space Travelers learn to fully understand that different facial features and body gestures can be representative of different emotions. Discuss with the Space Travelers how they know that a friend is happy with them, annoyed with them, disappointed with them, angry with them, worried about them, and so on. Concentrate on the body signals the friend may be giving them, along with the words being expressed.

Explain that the Alien Features activity delves into the facial features that may be associated with different emotions. No one facial feature is the right one for each emotion. Give a few examples using your own face; portray different emotions with your face and invite the Space Travelers to guess the emotion you are representing. You may choose to add whole-body language as well as thinking or speaking parts to your portrayal.

Directions:

The Space Travelers draw aliens' faces to show the facial expression that matches the emotion listed in each box (see example to the right). If time permits, the Space Travelers share their alien facial features with the crew.

CALM

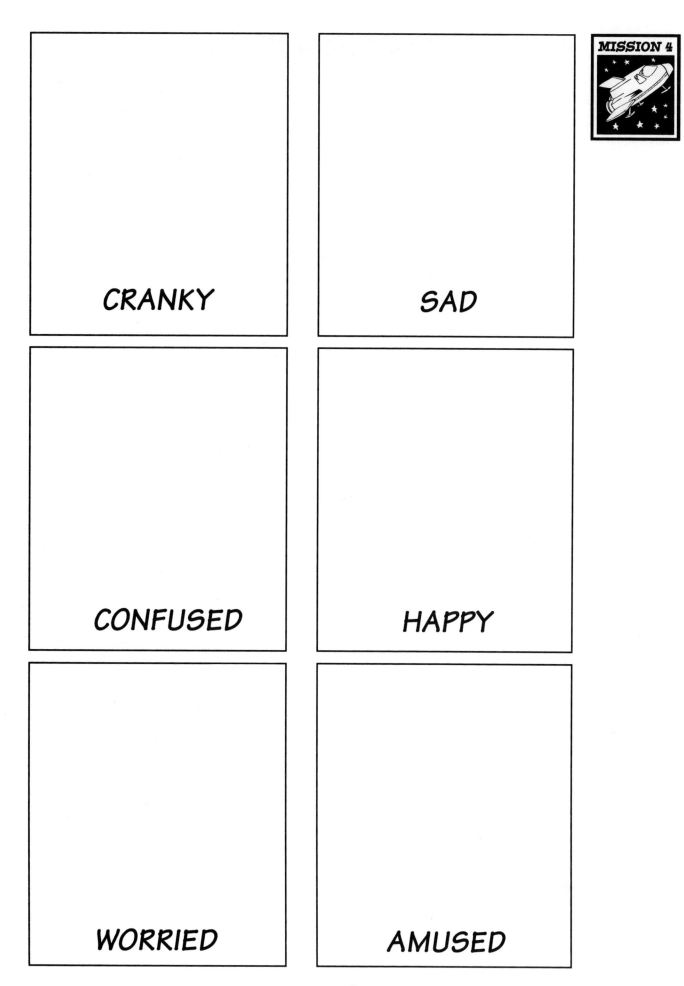

CRANKY

SAD

CONFUSED

HAPPY

WORRIED

AMUSED

MOTHER SHIP UPDATE

Hello Parents/Guardians,

This is your fourth Mother Ship Update. If you have any questions, please do not hesitate to contact me. My contact information is as follows:

Name: _____

Phone: _____

Fax: _____

E-mail: _____

Constellation Chart

MISSION 1

LAUNCH PAD

MISSION 2

INTRODUCING THE CREW

MISSION 3

STARLIGHT AND GRAVITY THINKING

MISSION 4

THE FEELINGS SHUTTLE

MISSION 5

ATMOSPHERIC PRESSURE

MISSION 6

MISSION CONTROL

MISSION 7

SPACE WALKING – PREPARING FOR LANDING

MISSION 8

TOUCHDOWN PARTY

MISSION 4

The goal for Mission 4 was to assist the Space Travelers in learning more about their own and others' emotions.

MISSION OUTCOMES
Students:

- Expanded their emotions vocabulary

- Deepened their awareness that everyone has emotions that are unique to him/herself

- Deepened their under-standing of different emotions

SPACE TRAVELER'S JOURNAL

MISSION 4

Date: _____

What I liked about today's mission:

New ideas I have learned:

What interested me most:

I'm curious about:

Actions I'm going to take:

SPACE GUIDE'S JOURNAL

This journal is completed by the Space Guide at the end of each mission to identify what went well with the mission, what was problematic, what was unexpected, what would be done differently if the mission was taught again, what questions came up during the mission, and so on.

Date: _____

What went well:

What was problematic:

What was unexpected:

What I would do differently if I taught this mission again:

What questions were raised for me during this mission:

Additional comments:

ATMOSPHERIC PRESSURE

Space Guide's Maintenance Checklist

MISSION AHEAD

Your goals as Space Guide for Mission 5 are to continue developing the Space Travelers' awareness and understanding of different emotions and the thinking and acting associated with each. You will also support the Space Travelers in learning more about how they respond to situations that trigger their angry emotions and understanding that they have a choice in their response to situations.

MISSION OUTCOMES

Space Travelers will:

☐ Broaden their repertoire of helpful ways of responding to angry emotions

☐ Learn more about the degrees of intensity associated with emotions

☐ Be introduced to the concept of the emotions thermometer

☐ Continue to learn that we have a choice about how we perceive situations (e.g., negative [pessimistic] or positive [optimistic])

☐ Reflect on their personal responses to angry emotions

MISSION LENGTH

1-1/2 hrs.

MISSION SUPPLIES

You will need the following:

☐ Space Traveler manual (one copy per Space Traveler)

☐ A collection of Asteroid Asks

☐ A rocket fuel tank

☐ Photocopies of Planet Cards (one set per pair of Space Travelers)

☐ Colored pencils/markers

☐ Paint and paint brushes

☐ Art paper

MISSION 5

☐ CD player

☐ Music (Temperatures Rising activity)

☐ Mother Ship Update (one copy per Space Traveler)

MISSION ITINERARY

Your itinerary for this mission is in two parts:

Part 1: Preparing to Launch – To Be Completed Before Mission 5 Begins

☐ Familiarize yourself with the content of Mission 5 (both from your manual and the Space Traveler manual).

☐ Photocopy Planet Cards (one set per pair of Space Travelers).

☐ Provide supplies and equipment listed for the Temperatures Rising activity.

Part 2: Launching Mission – Structure for Mission 5

☐ Welcome the Space Travelers.

☐ Referring to the constellation chart, introduce the purpose of the overall mission and explain the itinerary.

☐ Hand out the Space Traveler manuals.

☐ Revisit and reteach the rules agreed to in the space contract.

☐ Have the Space Travelers complete the Questron activity.

☐ Have the Space Travelers complete the Countdown activity.

☐ Have the Space Travelers complete the Planet Cards activity.

☐ Have the Space Travelers complete the Temperatures Rising activity.

☐ Have the Space Travelers complete the Tracking Station activity.

☐ Invite the Space Travelers to draw/write/dictate an Asteroid Asks.

☐ Answer the Asteroid Asks before the Space Travelers begin working on their space journal.

☐ Have the Space Travelers write/draw/dictate in their space journal.

☐ Hand out a Mother Ship Update to the Space Travelers to take home.

☐ Complete the Space Guide's journal.

MISSION 5 ACTIVITIES

Constellation Chart
A visual chart of the eight missions allowing the Space Travelers to plot their space journey. (Space Travelers decorate current mission.)

Space Traveler Contract
Rules agreed to in the space contract. (Revisit and reteach as needed.)

Questron
A self-reflection questionnaire that helps the Space Travelers to identify (a) the strategies they choose in responding to angry emotions and angry thinking; and (b) how helpful these strategies are.

Countdown
An activity where the Space Travelers match emotions with different intensity levels on a scale to broaden their understanding that individuals respond with different levels of intensity to the same emotion.

Planet Cards
A card game played in pairs in which the Space Travelers provide a creative story that links an emotion card with a story card selected from the deck of Planet Cards.

The purpose of this activity is to further deepen the Space Travelers' understanding of emotions connected with social scenarios. The connections may be quite unusual – the more out of the ordinary the connections are, the more imaginative the Space Traveler story becomes. The stories can be fantasy or reality, providing the Space Traveler with the opportunity to think outside the box.

Temperatures Rising
A creative art activity where the Space Travelers paint the emotions they feel when a particular piece of music is played. The intent is to help them experience and identify different emotional responses.

Tracking Station
A log where the Space Travelers record what happened in specific social situations and how they responded. This activity assists the Space Travelers in recognizing that their responses in social situations can either escalate or help calm their emotions. Once the logs are completed, debrief each Space Traveler, either on an individual basis or in pairs.

Asteroid Asks

A question-and-answer clarification activity. The Space Travelers are invited to write/draw/dictate a question on the Asteroid Ask card related to the current mission, whether a question about the mission overview, mission itinerary, and so on. Once completed, the Asteroid Asks are placed in the rocket fuel tank. The Space Guide responds to the Asteroid Asks before the Space Travelers begin to work on their space journals.

Space Journals

A journal that Space Travelers can write/draw/dictate in about what they learned during Mission 5.

Mother Ship Update

A newsletter for home explaining the goals and activities for Mission 5.

Space Guide Journal

A journal for the Space Guide to complete, identifying what went well with the mission, what was problematic, what was unexpected, what would be done differently if the mission was taught again, what questions came up and whether the intended outcomes were achieved.

QUESTRON

Discuss with the Space Travelers that everyone in the crew, just like everyone in the Mother Ship, responds differently when they are feeling angry. This is because we are all unique; our responses to our emotions are a key example of our individuality. Sometimes we know that our responses to our angry emotions are unhelpful because our anger

escalates and we become furious or/and enraged. At other times our responses are helpful because we deal with our angry emotions in constructive ways (e.g., take deep breaths and use assertive words rather than banging the walls and smashing the furniture).

This self-reflection activity provides the Space Travelers with an opportunity to think about what happens to them when they are at different stages of being angry. Their responses may help them to identify the strategies they use when responding to angry emotions and angry thinking. Information gleaned from this activity is a necessary springboard for other activities in this mission.

Once the Space Travelers have completed the Questron, discuss their information with them. Then have them draw pictures of the last time they got angry.

QUESTRON

Do all people have emotions? _____

Do all people show emotions in the same way? _____

What is the first thing someone notices about you when you are getting angry? _____

What do you do and what do you think about when you are angry? _____

_____

Do you calm down? _____

How do you calm down? _____

How do you know if someone else is angry? _____

_____

When was the last time you got angry? _____

77

QUESTRON cont.

Draw pictures of the last time you got angry.

Before you got angry.	Getting angry.
Being angry.	**What happened then?**

COUNTDOWN

Introduce the Space Travelers to the concept of "intensity" of emotions. Feeling calm and relaxed are low-intensity emotions on the scale of intensity compared to feeling furious and enraged, which are high-intensity emotions. The more extreme the emotions, the more intense  they are. Each Space Traveler may experience different levels of intensity for the same emotion. Also, while they may experience the same intensity level for the same emotion, they may behave in a completely different way in response.

This activity gives the Space Travelers the opportunity to record their own perception of the intensity level of different emotions. This information gives the Space Guide insight into the Space Travelers' tolerance for frustration, what emotion comes before another emotion on a scale from 1-10, and the intensity level they assign to each emotion.

Directions:

PART A
Complete Part A of the Countdown on your own.

1. Think about the different emotions named on the worksheet.

2. Think about the order you would place each emotion in, beginning at the bottom of the rocket at 1 and finishing at the top of the rocket at 10.

3. Draw a line matching the emotions on the right with the rising temperature of emotions on the left.

PART B
Complete Part B with the entire crew.

1. Compare your Countdown scale with the Countdown scales of other crew members.

10.   CALM

9.   IRRITATED

8.   ANNOYED

7.   FURIOUS

6.   AGITATED

5.   WORRIED

4.   ANGRY

3.   FRUSTRATED

2.   HAPPY

1.   EXPLOSIVE

PLANET CARDS

The Space Travelers play this game in pairs. Selecting both a space story card and an emotion card from a deck of Planet Cards, they formulate a creative connection between the two cards. The stories may

be based on reality or imagination. The more ingenious the connections, the more amusing the story.

Directions:

1. Find a crew member to play Planet Cards with.

2. Your Space Guide will give you a deck of cards. Separate the emotion cards from the story cards.

3. Arrange the emotion cards in a deck and place them between you and your partner.

4. Deal out the story cards so that you and your partner have four each.

5. Spread out your story cards in front of you so the other crew member also can see them.

6. Decide who will go first.

7. Whoever goes first chooses one of four story cards and reads it.

8. Then, the same person selects an emotion card from the top of the deck.

9. Finally, whoever goes first creates a connection between the story card and the emotion written on the emotion card. For example, you select FRUSTRATED (emotion card) and "You are tripped over on purpose by an alien" (story card).

10. Now, link the emotion card with the space story card. In your story, you may explain that you felt frustrated because you knew the alien did it on purpose and you hadn't done anything to annoy him.

PLANET CARDS cont.

Emotion Cards

CALM
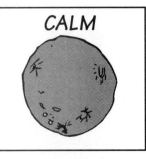

ANGRY

HAPPY

FURIOUS

IRRITATED

WORRIED

FRUSTRATED

EXPLOSIVE

AGITATED
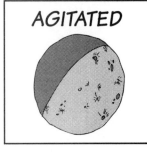

ANNOYED

Story Cards

You are lost in space

You are going to the space cinema to see "Space Invaders"

You are going on a space walk

One of the Space Travelers keeps teasing you about your space boots

You were not chosen to play space soccer

You have hurt your foot and cannot space walk with the others

An alien trips you over on purpose

Somebody has accused you of cheating in the space game, when you know you've played fair

A space creature stole your space snack

You have received a consequence of not being allowed to join the other Space Travelers in a sleepover on the planet Saturn

82

TEMPERATURES RISING

Music is considered a powerful medium for communicating emotions and feelings. In Temperatures Rising, play a variety of background music and invite the Space Travelers to paint images, emotions and feelings that they associate with the music. Encourage them to focus on both the explosive and the serene parts of the music being played.

When the music stops, discuss the emotions and feelings evoked by the different pieces of music. Invite the Space Travelers to share their paintings with the crew.

TRACKING STATION

Introduce the Tracking Station to the Space Travelers, explaining that it is a visual way of helping them keep track of how they are dealing with social conflicts. Are their responses helpful and within the school rules, or are they unhelpful and in violation of the school rules? It is important to demonstrate how to complete a Tracking Station questionnaire before asking the Space Travelers to complete one on their own.

The Space Travelers complete this self-reflection questionnaire, recording their perception of what happened in a given social situation and how they chose to respond. Discuss their completed Tracking Station questionnaire with the Space Travelers on an individual basis. This discussion will provide you with valuable insight into how each Space Traveler perceives social conflicts and his or her personal response to the conflict.

TRACKING STATION cont.

Name: _____ Date: _____

Where was I?

☐ classroom ☐ playground ☐ restrooms ☐ other

What happened?

☐ He/she teased me
☐ He/she took something that belongs to me without asking
☐ He/she told me to do something I didn't want to do
☐ I started fighting with him/her
☐ I chose not to follow the class/school rules
☐ I told him/her to do something and he/she didn't do it
☐ Other

Who was involved?

☐ classmate   ☐ teacher   ☐ family member
☐ another adult   ☐ stranger   ☐ other

What did you do?

☐ hit back   ☐ ran away   ☐ shouted
☐ cried   ☐ broke something   ☐ walked away calmly
☐ talked it out   ☐ told an adult   ☐ told a peer
☐ took deep breaths ☐ ignored it   ☐ other

How angry were you?

☐ Not angry   ☐ A little angry   ☐ Quite angry   ☐ Very angry

Was what you did helpful or unhelpful? _____

What other helpful choices could you have made? _____

_____

What will you do differently next time? _____

_____

The Space Travelers can use the Tracking Station outside of each mission as a way of helping them keep track of how successful they are in dealing with social conflicts.

MOTHER SHIP UPDATE

Hello Parents/Guardians,

This is your fifth Mother Ship Update. If you have any questions, please do not hesitate to contact me. My contact information is as follows:

Name: _____

Phone: _____

Fax: _____

E-mail: _____

Constellation Chart

MISSION 1

LAUNCH PAD

MISSION 5

ATMOSPHERIC PRESSURE

MISSION 2

INTRODUCING THE CREW

MISSION 6

MISSION CONTROL

MISSION 3

STARLIGHT AND GRAVITY THINKING

MISSION 7

SPACE WALKING – PREPARING FOR LANDING

MISSION 4

THE FEELINGS SHUTTLE

MISSION 8

TOUCHDOWN PARTY

MISSION 5

The goals for Mission 5 were to (a) continue developing the Space Travelers' awareness and understanding of angry emotions and the thinking and acting associated with each; and (b) to support Space Travelers in learning more about how they respond to situations that trigger their angry emotions and show them that they have a choice in their response to various situations.

MISSION OUTCOMES
Students:

- Broadened their repertoire of helpful ways of responding to angry emotions

- Learned more about the degrees of intensity associated with emotions

- Learned the concept of the emotions thermometer

- Learned that we have a choice about how we perceive situations (e.g., negative [pessimistic] or positive [optimistic])

- Reflected on angry emotions and possible alternatives

86

SPACE TRAVELER'S JOURNAL

Date: _____

What I liked about today's mission:

New ideas I have learned:

What interested me most:

I'm curious about:

Actions I'm going to take:

MISSION 5

SPACE GUIDE'S JOURNAL

This journal is completed by the Space Guide at the end of each mission to identify what went well with the mission, what was problematic, what was unexpected, what would be done differently if the mission was taught again, what questions came up during the mission, and so on.

Date: _____

What went well:

What was problematic:

What was unexpected:

What I would do differently if I taught this mission again:

What questions were raised for me during this mission:

Additional comments:

MISSION CONTROL
SPACE GUIDE'S
MAINTENANCE CHECKLIST

MISSION AHEAD

Your goal as Space Guide for Mission 6 is to continue teaching the Space Travelers peaceful and positive ways of working and playing together. In this mission you focus on social problem solving with a continuing emphasis on exploring self-calming strategies.

MISSION OUTCOMES

Space Travelers will:

☐ Become familiar with the STOP, THINK, CHOOSE, DO social problem-solving process

☐ Identify and discuss various self-calming strategies

☐ Learn the invisible shield technique

MISSION LENGTH

2 hrs.

MISSION SUPPLIES

You will need the following:

☐ Space Traveler manual (one copy per Space Traveler)

☐ A collection of Asteroid Asks

☐ A rocket fuel tank

☐ Photocopies of Lunar Marks (one per Space Traveler)

☐ Scissors, colored pencils/markers

☐ Photocopies of Stellar Stories (one per Space Traveler)

☐ Photocopies of Antenna Ask cards for the host (Space Guide) of the Galaxy Panel quiz game

☐ Mother Ship Update (one copy per Space Traveler). Please give your contact information in the space provided prior to copying

MISSION ITINERARY

Your itinerary for this mission is in two parts:

Part 1: Preparing to Launch – To Be Completed Before Mission 6 Begins

☐ Familiarize yourself with the content of Mission 6 (both from your manual and the Space Traveler manual).

☐ Photocopy Lunar Marks (one per Space Traveler).

☐ Photocopy Stellar Stories (one per Space Traveler) and cut out.

☐ Photocopy Antenna Ask cards (for the host) and cut out.

Part 2: Launching Mission – Structure for Mission 6

☐ Welcome the Space Travelers.

☐ Referring to the constellation chart, introduce the purpose of the overall mission and explain the itinerary.

☐ Hand out the Space Traveler manuals and collect at the end of the session.

☐ Revisit and reteach the rules agreed to in the space contract.

☐ Have the Space Travelers complete the Personal Force-Field activity.

☐ Have the Space Travelers complete the Data Signals activity.

☐ Have the Space Travelers complete the Lunar Marks activity.

☐ Have the Space Travelers complete the Galaxy Panel activity.

☐ Have the Space Travelers complete the Antenna Asks activity.

☐ Have the Space Travelers complete the Asteroid Asks activity.

☐ Have the Space Travelers complete the Stellar Stories activity.

☐ Invite the Space Travelers to draw/write/dictate an Asteroid Ask.

☐ Answer the Asteroid Asks before the Space Travelers begin working on their space journal.

☐ Have the Space Travelers write/draw/dictate in their space journal.

☐ Hand out a Mother Ship Update to the Space Travelers to take home.

☐ Complete the Space Guide's journal.

MISSION 6 ACTIVITIES

Constellation Chart
A visual chart of the eight missions allowing the Space Travelers to plot their space journey. (Space Travelers decorate current mission.)

Space Traveler Contract
Rules agreed to in the space contract. (Revisit and reteach as needed.)

Personal Force-Field
A practical strategy for the Space Travelers to use to deflect put-downs. Put-downs have the potential of triggering angry feelings and angry thinking.

Data Signals
A role-play activity where the Space Travelers discuss and role-play helpful ways of calming down when their angry emotions are triggered.

Lunar Marks
An activity where the Space Travelers design their own STOP, THINK, CHOOSE, DO calm-down plan in the form of a bookmark.

Galaxy Panel
A quiz game played in four teams using the STOP, THINK, CHOOSE, DO social problem-solving strategy.

Antenna Asks
A creative solutions game where the Space Travelers are given a social scenario and as a team identify one helpful and one unhelpful response to the scenario. The Space Travelers then explain why they would classify their responses as either helpful or unhelpful. That is, what their criteria are for saying that one response was helpful and another was unhelpful.

Stellar Stories
A cooperative crew activity where the Space Travelers work together to solve social situations using the STOP, THINK, CHOOSE and DO social problem-solving strategy.

Asteroid Asks
A question-and-answer clarification activity. The Space Travelers are invited to write/draw/dictate a question on the Asteroid Ask card related to the current mission, whether a question about the mission overview, mission itinerary, and so on. Once completed, the Asteroid Asks are placed in the rocket fuel tank. The Space Guide responds to the Asteroid Asks before the Space Travelers begin to work on their space journals.

Space Journals
A journal that Space Travelers can write/draw in about what they learned during Mission 6.

Mother Ship Update
A newsletter for home explaining the goals and activities for Mission 6.

Space Guide Journal
A journal for the Space Guide to complete, identifying what went well with the mission, what was problematic, what was unexpected, what would be done differently if the mission was taught again, what questions came up and whether the intended outcomes were achieved.

PERSONAL FORCE-FIELD

Talk with the Space Travelers about the signals our bodies receive when we experience different emotions. Explain that even if each of us experiences the same situation, we may respond very differently. We may think about it differently, feel it differently and respond to it differently.

Discuss with the Space Travelers the body signals they receive when they are feeling calm compared to when they are feeling annoyed, frustrated, angry, and so on. Compare and contrast body signals. Emphasize that everyone has his or her own signals and intensity of signals. That is one of the things that make us unique!

Introduce the Personal Force-Field concept. This is a practical strategy that Space Travelers can apply when they notice that their body signals are changing from being calm to being annoyed, frustrated, angry, and so on.

Directions:

When you have calm feelings, what is your body doing?

When you have annoyed feelings, what is your body doing?

When you have happy feelings, what is your body doing?

When you have worried feelings, what is your body doing?

When you have angry feelings, what is your body doing?

Does your body feel explosive, like it is tense, taut, tight, jittery, frazzled, sore or achy?

On the Personal Force-Field worksheet, circle the parts of your body where you feel your angry feelings.

It's OK to have angry feelings. Just make sure you choose a helpful way to deal with your angry feelings.

Let me introduce you to your Personal Force-Field.

- You can choose to use your Personal Force-Field to bounce off what sparks your angry feelings.

- Your Personal Force-Field is an invisible field you imagine surrounding your body. It is always there for you to use.

- Nobody else but you can see and control your Personal Force-Field.

- Take turns with the crew to practice using your Personal Force-Field.

Monitor the Space Travelers' understanding of the strategy and their application of it during this activity.

PERSONAL FORCE-FIELD cont.

DATA SIGNALS

Discuss with the crew helpful ways of responding to angering emotions and angry thinking. Talk with them about the difference between helpful and unhelpful ways of responding, and the importance of learning helpful and constructive ways of responding to emotions and feelings. Assist the Space Travelers in coming up with preferred strategies of responding to their angry emotions and thinking.

1. Role-play each strategy with the Space Travelers so that they become more than words on a page.

2. Reflect with the crew on their dramatizations of preferred strategies.

CALMING STRATEGIES

- Ignore
- Walk away
- Take deep breaths
- Count quietly to 10
- Think about staying calm
- Talk to someone
- Use a crazy compliment
- Think about a helpful thing to do
- Fold my arms
- Talk to my friends
- Say, "I don't like that"

MISSION 6

LUNAR MARKS

Introduce and explain the STOP, THINK, CHOOSE, DO problem-solving strategy. You can expand on the information the Space Travelers discussed and learned in the Data Signals activity earlier in this mission. The purpose of the present activity is to (a) teach the Space Travelers the reason for and the composition of a STOP, THINK, CHOOSE, DO plan; and (b) have the Space Travelers visually record their personal STOP, THINK, CHOOSE, DO plan in the form of a LUNAR MARK.

Explain what each part of the STOP, THINK, CHOOSE, DO plan represents.

STOP   =   Stop everything so you are free to think of your
                     strategies to calm down.
THINK   =   Think of three helpful calming choices from the list below.
CHOOSE =   Choose from these calming choices.
DO   =   Try out your calm-down plan.

Explain to the Space Travelers that they will have an opportunity to create their own STOP, THINK, CHOOSE, DO calm-down plan. Brainstorm helpful and constructive calm-down strategies that the Space Travelers can use when their angering emotions are escalating. Record all responses.

Examples may include the following:

- Take yourself to time-out
- Scream in the garage
- Tell yourself, "Keep calm"
- Keep your hands to yourself
- Write in your diary

- Take deep breaths
- Go for a run
- Walk away
- Jump up and down
- Close your eyes and think of your favorite thing to do

- Count to 10
- Listen to music
- Tell someone
- Punch your pillow

Ask the Space Travelers to think about all of these strategies and to select three or four that they think would be most useful for them. These may be strategies they are using now or strategies they have not used before. Ask the Space Travelers to include these strategies in their calm-down plans.

It is now time for the Space Travelers to formulate a draft STOP, THINK, CHOOSE, DO plan. Ask them to share their draft plan with two other Space Travelers and make changes to their plan as necessary.

The Space Travelers now visually record their draft STOP, THINK, CHOOSE, DO plan on their Lunar Mark card. Provide them each with a "bookmark" outline and ask them to record their calm-down plan in a sequence on it. Explain that the reason for recording the plan as a bookmark is to help them remember to follow their plan. Whenever they look at their bookmark, they will be reminded of their plan.

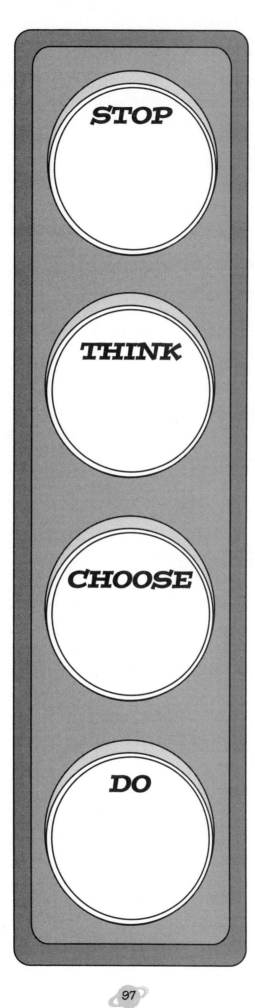

STOP

THINK

CHOOSE

DO

GALAXY PANEL

The Galaxy Plan provides the Space Travelers with an opportunity to work as teams, each team representing one aspect of the STOP, THINK, CHOOSE, DO problem-solving plan. As host, explain the rules and procedures of the Galaxy Panel quiz game to the crew.

The Space Travelers form four teams (equal numbers in each team), for example:

- SOLAR WINGS
- TRANSMITTERS
- SATELLITES
- SKY-LABS

The Space Guide nominates which team is the STOP, THINK, CHOOSE and DO teams for the first round. Each team will have a turn being the STOP, THINK, CHOOSE and DO team, respectively.

The host reads the scenario from an Antenna Ask card (see page 99).

Each team huddles together separately to work out their action to the scenario as follows.

- STOP team shouts "STOP," indicating it's the THINK teams turn.
- THINK team names helpful and unhelpful ways of reacting to the scenario (e.g., throwing a tantrum/playing somewhere else/asking for help).
- CHOOSE team names the most helpful choice for the scenario (e.g., asking for help).
- DO team follows through on the choice by role-playing.

The Space Guide rotates the teams until everybody has had a chance to be on the STOP, THINK, CHOOSE, or DO teams.

ANTENNA ASKS

MISSION 6

Before the game begins, the Space Travelers decide who will be Space Traveler Q – the person who provides responses to the Antenna Asks – and Space Traveler Z – the person who provides the reasons supporting Space Traveler Q's responses. Space Travelers work in pairs, with one providing the response (Space Traveler Q) and the other (Space Traveler Z) giving the reason why the responses were either helpful or unhelpful.

As the host, the Space Guide reads out the Antenna Asks social scenario. Space Traveler Q identifies one helpful and one unhelpful way of behaving to the Antenna Asks scenario. Space Traveler Z then offers supporting reasons for Space Traveler Q's responses. Space Travelers Q and Z can work together formulating answers to the Antenna Asks and the reasons why they are either helpful or unhelpful.

Before the game begins, give an example of how to play the game. Identify what would be classified as a helpful response and what would be classified as an unhelpful response. Provide supporting reasons for each response. After modeling how the game is played, ask two Space Travelers to role-play how to play the game. Emphasize the teaming aspect of the game; that is, the Space Travelers can support one another in their roles.

Sample Antenna Asks Social Scenarios:

You lose your new space helmet.

An alien pushes you over for no reason.

You want to play three-dimensional space chess but your friends don't want you to play.

An alien copies your space project and gets a better mark than you do.

Make up additional Antenna Asks relevant to social problems encountered by Space Travelers in your particular group.

99

From Carter, M., & Santomauro, J. (2004). *Space travelers.* Shawnee Mission, KS: Autism Asperger Publishing Company. Copied with permission.

MISSION 6

STELLAR STORIES

Facilitate this cooperative team activity, reading out the plot and the sentence starter. Encourage the Space Travelers to be as inventive as possible with the plot, including different circumstances where the STOP, THINK, CHOOSE, DO problem-solving plan nearly resolves the situation, but not quite. The story is concluded when the STOP, THINK, CHOOSE, DO plan finally comes about.

Weaving story lines together is the key to the Stellar Stories. The Space Travelers take turns continuing to weave helpful STOP, THINK, CHOOSE, and DO strategies into the story plots.

STELLAR STORIES cont.

PLOT:

At snack time, an alien takes your space food. You are very annoyed because this is the only food you had in your cosmos case.

STARTER:

At snack time, Somsoc, the alien from planet Rewot, came over to me and . . .

_____

_____

PLOT:

When you go home to the Mother Ship, you are asked to clean your cabin. You don't want to clean your cabin because you want to play your favorite space game.

STARTER:

I went home to my Mother Ship yesterday and

_____

_____

PLOT:

Magella dares you to climb the transmitter tower. You know this is dangerous but don't want to look uncool.

STARTER:

This morning Magella said, "Hey, you wanna climb the transmitter tower?"

_____

_____

PLOT:

You sleep through your siren and are late for space walking class. Now you will have to miss out until the next lunar year.

STARTER:

I can't believe it! My stupid siren didn't go off this morning and . . .

_____

_____

MOTHER SHIP UPDATE

Hello Parents/Guardians,

This is your sixth Mother Ship Update. If you have any questions, please do not hesitate to contact me. My contact information is as follows:

Name: _____

Phone: _____

Fax: _____

E-mail: _____

Constellation Chart

MISSION 6

The goal for Mission 6 was to continue teaching the Space Travelers peaceful and positive ways of working and playing together. In this mission we focused on social problem solving and continued to explore self-calming strategies.

MISSION OUTCOMES

Students:

🌏 Developed some familiarity with the STOP, THINK, CHOOSE, DO social problem-solving process

🌏 Identified and discussed various self-calming strategies

🌏 Learned the invisible shield technique

SPACE TRAVELER'S JOURNAL

Date: _____

What I liked about today's mission:

New ideas I have learned:

What interested me most:

I'm curious about:

Actions I'm going to take:

MISSION 6

SPACE GUIDE'S JOURNAL

This journal is completed by the Space Guide at the end of each mission to identify what went well with the mission, what was problematic, what was unexpected, what would be done differently if the mission was taught again, what questions came up during the mission, and so on.

Date: _____

What went well:

What was problematic:

What was unexpected:

What I would do differently if I taught this mission **again**:

What questions were raised for me during this mission:

Additional comments:

SPACE WALKING – PREPARING FOR LANDING

SPACE GUIDE'S MAINTENANCE CHECKLIST

MISSION AHEAD

Your goals as Space Guide for Mission 7 are to teach the Space Travelers more relaxation strategies, to identify positive ways of responding in social situations and to prepare for the end of the journey.

MISSION OUTCOMES

Space Travelers will:

☐ Participate in and reflect on the Space Walk 2 visualization activity

☐ Identify and share positive ways of responding to social situations

☐ Prepare for the Touchdown Party

MISSION LENGTH

1-1/2 hrs.

MISSION SUPPLIES

You will need the following:

☐ Space Traveler manual (one copy per Space Traveler)

☐ A collection of Asteroid Asks

☐ A rocket fuel tank

☐ Photocopies of Touchdown Party Plan (one per Space Traveler)

☐ Photocopies of Touchdown Party Invitation (one per Space Traveler)

☐ Scissors, colored pencils/markers

☐ Dictionary (one per Space Traveler)

☐ Decorative materials (e.g., glitter)

☐ Mother Ship Update (one copy per Space Traveler)

MISSION ITINERARY

Your itinerary for this mission is in two parts.

Part 1: Preparing to Launch – To Be Completed Before Mission 7 Begins

☐ Familiarize yourself with the content of Mission 7 (both from your manual and the Space Traveler manual).

☐ Photocopy Touchdown Party Plan (one per Space Traveler).

☐ Photocopy Touchdown Party Invitation (one per Space Traveler).

☐ Provide decorative materials for invitation.

Part 2: Launching Mission – Structure for Mission 7

☐ Welcome the Space Travelers.

☐ Referring to the constellation chart, introduce the purpose of the overall mission and explain the itinerary.

☐ Hand out the Space Traveler manuals and collect them at the end of the session.

☐ Revisit the space contract.

☐ Have the Space Travelers complete the Space Walk 2 activity.

☐ Have the Space Travelers complete the Galactic Center activity.

☐ Have the Space Travelers complete the Simulation activity.

☐ Have the Space Travelers complete the Space Food activity.

☐ Have the Space Travelers complete the Touchdown Party Invitation activity.

☐ Invite the Space Travelers to draw/write/dictate an Asteroid Ask.

☐ Answer the Asteroid Asks before the Space Travelers begin working on their space journal.

☐ Have the Space Travelers write/draw/dictate in their space journal.

☐ Hand out a Mother Ship Update to the Space Travelers to take home.

☐ Complete the Space Guide's journal.

MISSION 7 ACTIVITIES

Constellation Chart
A visual chart of the eight missions allowing the Space Travelers to plot their space journey. (Space Travelers decorate current mission.)

Space Traveler Contract
Rules agreed to in the space contract. (Revisit and reteach as needed.)

Space Walk 2
A meditation activity in which the Space Travelers embark on a visualization journey focusing on raising their awareness of how their body feels in this meditative state.

Galactic Center
An acrostic poem that the Space Travelers complete, identifying positive and constructive ways of responding to social situations.

Simulation
A collaborative activity in which the Space Travelers and the Space Guide prepare for the Touchdown Party, Mission 8.

Space Food
A negotiation activity involving Space Travelers and the Space Guide to plan the menu for the Touchdown Party, Mission 8.

Touchdown Party Invitations
A creative activity in which the Space Travelers design their Touchdown Party Invitation for the Mother Ship.

Asteroid Asks
A question-and-answer clarification activity. The Space Travelers are invited to write/draw/dictate a question on the Asteroid Ask card related to the current mission, whether a question about the mission overview, mission itinerary, and so on. Once completed, the Asteroid Asks are placed in the rocket fuel tank. The Space Guide responds to the Asteroid Asks before the Space Travelers begin to work on their space journals.

Space Journals
A journal that Space Travelers can write/draw/dictate in about what they learned during Mission 7.

Mother Ship Update
A newsletter for home explaining the goals and activities for Mission 7.

Space Guide Journal
A journal for the Space Guide to complete, identifying what went well with the mission, what was problematic, what was unexpected, what would be done differently if the mission was taught again, what questions came up and whether the intended outcomes were achieved.

SPACE WALK 2

This is a relaxation, visualization activity where you as Space Guide read the following visualization script to the Space Travelers. Review with the Space Travelers what a visualization is: creating a mental picture of the words being spoken/scene being described, imagining in your mind the scene being described/script being read. Remind the Space Travelers of their Space Walk 1 visualization in Mission 1. Invite them to review the drawing of the visualization they made in Mission 1.

After the Space Walk 2 visualization, invite the Space Travelers to draw their visualization and to share their drawing with two other Space Travelers. Provide prompts if required.

SPACE WALK 2 Script:

You are an astronaut about to embark on a space walk outside of your spacecraft. To participate in this mission, you must first reach a completely relaxed state so your body can slip into the specially fitted space suit. You are standing in the airlock of the spacecraft. (Pause)

Close your eyes. (Pause) To reach this super-relaxed state you must focus on your breathing. Don't change your breathing; (Pause) just listen to your breath and breathe in and out as you would normally do. (Pause) As you breathe out, say to yourself the word "relax." Breathe in and then breathe out saying the word "relax" to yourself. (Allow a minute for the Space Travelers to practice.)

You are now ready to be placed into your space suit. The Space Engineer* helps you into your suit. Once you are fitted into your space suit and helmet, the Space Engineer exits the airlock and a hatch closes behind you. You are alone in the airlock. (Pause) You can hear a hissing noise as the air is being pumped out of the airlock. (Pause) Now we will start a countdown from 10 to 1. (Pause) When we reach the number 1, you will be in a super-relaxed state in your space suit and be ready to space walk.

10. You feel your whole body start to melt into the space suit. (Pause)
9. You feel your body sinking into the suit's various compartments. (Pause)
8. You feel your eyes, mouth and face relax. (Pause)
7. You feel your neck muscles relax. (Pause)
6. You feel your arms become heavy. (Pause)
5. You feel your stomach relax. (Pause)
4. You feel your legs turn jelly-like. (Pause)
3. You feel your feet relax. (Pause)
2. You are in a completely relaxed state. (Pause)
1. You are in a super-relaxed and calm state. (Pause)

*The person who takes the children on their space walk. This could be an OT/PT, an aide or anybody else with the prerequisite skills.

Your body is limp and like jelly. (Pause) Now your body is a perfect fit with your space suit and you are ready to exit the airlock. A hatch slides open and you step into space. (Pause) You are floating but you are attached to your spacecraft with a safety line. Imagine that you are floating in space and can do somersaults and cartwheels. (Pause) You can see your fellow Space Travelers with their space suits and helmets on. (Pause) You can see the stars, the planets and earth. (Pause) I will leave you for a few minutes to have some fun, and when it's time to go back into the spacecraft I will call you.

(Allow a few minutes.)

Now it is time to go back into your spacecraft. (Pause) Say goodbye to the other Space Travelers. (Pause) Have a last look around at the stars, planets and earth. (Pause) The hatch opens. (Pause) You step into the airlock. (Pause) The hatch closes behind you. The air is pumped back into the airlock. (Pause)

You remove your helmet.

The Space Engineer helps you out of your suit. (Pause)

You are now ready to come back into the space ship.

Open your eyes and wriggle your fingers and toes.

Welcome back!

Prompts for Drawings for Visualization Activity:

🐞 You are an astronaut about to embark on a space walk outside of your spacecraft wearing your specially fitted space suit and helmet

🐞 You are standing in the airlock of the spacecraft

🐞 You are alone in the airlock waiting to go on your space walk

🐞 You are exiting the airlock

🐞 You are floating in space attached to your spacecraft with a safety line

🐞 You are doing somersaults and cartwheels in space

🐞 You are looking at your fellow Space Travelers with their space suits and helmets on

🐞 You are looking at the stars, the planets and earth

🐞 You are having fun in space

🐞 You are returning to your space ship

GALACTIC CENTER

Explain to the Space Travelers that they are to devise an acrostic poem using the words "Galactic Center." The theme of the poem is positive and constructive strategies (Starlight thinking) for responding in social situations. Strategies may be ones the Space Travelers learned during their space mission or they may come from dictionaries. Give an example of how to complete an acrostic poem using a different phrase and perhaps even a different theme.

Example:

Using the letters from the word "blastoff," model for the Space Travelers an acrostic poem with the theme of how to stay calm.

*B*LOW BUBBLES
*L*AUGH
*A*CTIVITIES WITH FRIENDS
*S*TAY IN OWN SPACE
*T*EMPERATURE GAUGE
*O*UTLET SAFE
*F*AST RUN
*F*OLLOW PLAN

Once the Space Travelers have completed their acrostic poems, ask them to share them with the rest of the crew.

G _____

A _____

L _____

A _____

C _____

T _____

I _____

C _____

C _____

E _____

N _____

T _____

E _____

R _____

SIMULATION

The Space Travelers work collaboratively with the Space Guide to plan the details of the Touchdown Party. It is important that you as Space Guide facilitate the discussion to ensure that all Space Travelers have an equal chance of contributing and that all details are taken care of.

Brainstorm with the Space Travelers what food and drink, space crew games and decorations to have at the space-themed Touchdown Party. Identify space names to represent food, drinks, games and decorations.

Start with the food and drink. When Space Travelers contribute an idea, record it and see what space descriptor may be used (e.g., decorated iced cookies – UFOS). Make sure there is a good balance of food and drink and that Space Travelers with allergies are taken into consideration.

Move on to the space crew games. Make sure that all games are cooperative, fun, participatory and noncompetitive.

Finally, discuss space-themed decorations that the Space Travelers can assemble with minimal time and energy.

Once everything has been discussed and agreed to, develop a crew record of what each Space Traveler will be responsible for in terms of food and drink; that is, who will be bringing what food and what drink for the party. This information is recorded by each Space Traveler on his or her Space Food Touchdown Party Plan, which the Space Travelers take home to discuss with their parents/guardians.

The suggestions for food, drinks, games and decorations are only a guide. You may wish to add/delete, and so on.

SIMULATION cont.

FOOD and DRINK

UFOS	–	Decorated iced cookies
METEORITE CAKES	–	Decorated cupcakes
SPACE CHIP CRACKLES	–	Similar to chocolate "crackles" served in silver foil
SANDWICH STARS	–	Sandwiches cut into star shapes
SOLAR SWEETS	–	Mars bars, Milky Ways, space-shaped lollipops
SPACE SHAKES	–	Flavored milks
FIZZY FUEL	–	Soft drinks

_____

_____

SPACE CREW GAMES

MUSICAL METEORS	–	Musical chairs
ALIEN ANTICS	–	Three-legged races
STAR SEARCH	–	Lollipop hunt
GRAVITY GLOBULES	–	Blowing bubbles

_____

_____

DECORATIONS

Sparkly stars
Glitter
Artwork from the journey on display

_____

_____

SPACE FOOD

This is an individual activity in which you meet with each Space Traveler and plan his or her food/drink contribution to the Touchdown Party menu. It is important that each Space Traveler completes the party plan and takes it home.

TOUCHDOWN PARTY PLAN

The party food/drink is called:

_____

The ingredients are:

_____

_____

_____

I will need to make _____ (amount/quantity) of my party food.

I will ask _____ to help me prepare my party food.

Draw a picture of your party food below.

REMEMBER TO BRING YOUR PARTY FOOD TO MISSION 8!

TOUCHDOWN PARTY
INVITATION

To: _____

Space Travelers
invite you to
celebrate our
TOUCHDOWN!

DATE: _____

STARTING TIME: _____

FINISHING TIME: _____

LOCATION: _____

RSVP BY: _____

MOTHER SHIP UPDATE

MISSION 7

Hello Parents/Guardians,

This is your seventh Mother Ship Update. If you have any questions, please do not hesitate to contact me. My contact information is as follows:

Name: _____

Phone: _____

Fax: _____

E-mail: _____

MISSION 7

The goals for Mission 7 were (a) to learn more relaxation strategies, (b) to identify positive ways of responding in social situations and (c) to prepare for the end of the Space Travelers' journey.

MISSION OUTCOMES

Students:

- Participated in and reflected on the Space Walk 2 visualization

- Identified and shared positive ways of responding to social situations

- Prepared for the Touchdown Party

Constellation Chart

MISSION 1

LAUNCH PAD

MISSION 5

ATMOSPHERIC PRESSURE

MISSION 2

INTRODUCING THE CREW

MISSION 6

MISSION CONTROL

MISSION 3

STARLIGHT AND GRAVITY THINKING

MISSION 7

SPACE WALKING – PREPARING FOR LANDING

MISSION 4

THE FEELINGS SHUTTLE

MISSION 8

TOUCHDOWN PARTY

115

SPACE TRAVELER'S JOURNAL

Date: _____

What I liked about today's mission:

New ideas I have learned:

What interested me most:

I'm curious about:

Actions I'm going to take:

SPACE GUIDE'S JOURNAL

This journal is completed by the Space Guide at the end of each mission to identify what went well with the mission, what was problematic, what was unexpected, what would be done differently if the mission was taught again, what questions came up during the mission, and so on.

Date: _____

What went well:

What was problematic:

What was unexpected:

What I would do differently if I taught this mission again:

What questions were raised for me during this mission:

Additional comments:

TOUCHDOWN PARTY
SPACE GUIDE'S
MAINTENANCE CHECKLIST

MISSION AHEAD

Your goals as Space Guide for Mission 8 are to support the Space Travelers in reflecting on their space journey and in celebrating what they have learned during the journey.

MISSION OUTCOMES

Space Travelers will:

- [ ] Review the social understanding gained during the space journey
- [ ] Celebrate working together as a crew during the space journey
- [ ] Share social understanding learned during the space journey

MISSION SUPPLIES

You will need the following:

- [ ] Space Traveler manuals (one copy per Space Traveler)
- [ ] Photocopies of the space graduation certificate on colored paper/ cardstock (one per Space Traveler)
- [ ] Materials gathered from each mission to be displayed (e.g., constellation chart, space suit, temperatures rising, etc.)
- [ ] Mother Ship Update (one copy per Space Traveler)

MISSION LENGTH and ITINERARY

2 hrs.

1st half hour: Mission Basics

- [ ] Welcome the Space Travelers.
- [ ] Referring to the constellation chart, introduce the purpose of the overall mission and explain the itinerary.
- [ ] Hand out the Space Traveler manuals.
- [ ] Revisit and reteach the rules agreed to in the space contract.
- [ ] Do the Observatorium activity.

MISSION 8

2nd half hour: Set up for Touchdown Party, including:

- ☐ Decorations
- ☐ Displays
- ☐ Food and drink
- ☐ Games

3rd half hour: Party

- ☐ Welcome guests.
- ☐ Introduce the Space Travelers by presenting them with their graduation certificate.
- ☐ Ask the Space Travelers to identify one concept they have learned during the space journey.
- ☐ PARTY!

4th half hour: Winding Down

- ☐ Clean up.
- ☐ Have the Space Travelers write/draw/dictate in the space journal.
- ☐ Have the Space Travelers sign autographs in the Space Traveler manuals.
- ☐ Hand out the final Mother Ship Update to each Space Traveler.
- ☐ Complete the Space Guide's journal.

MISSION 8 ACTIVITIES

Constellation Chart
A visual chart of the eight missions allowing the Space Travelers to plot their space journey. (Space Travelers decorate current mission.)

Space Traveler Contract
Rules agreed to in Mission 1. (Revisit and reteach as needed.)

Observatorium
A self-reflection activity where the Space Travelers respond to questions specific to their experiences throughout the space journey.

Touchdown Party
A celebration of having completed the space journey.

Space Graduation Certificate
A graduation certificate recognizing the Space Travelers' effort and participation during the space journey.

Autographs
Space Travelers signing their names in the autograph section of each other's manual.

Space Journals
A journal that Space Travelers can write/draw/dictate in about what they learned during Mission 8.

Mother Ship Update
A newsletter for home explaining the goals and activities for Mission 8.

Space Guide Journal
A journal for the Space Guide to complete, identifying what went well with the mission, what was problematic, what was unexpected, what would be done differently if the mission was taught again, what questions came up and whether the intended outcomes were achieved.

OBSERVATORIUM

Introduce the Observatorium to the Space Travelers, explaining that information gathered from a completed Observatorium is one way for them to review what they have learned during the eight-week space mission. It also provides an opportunity for the Space Travelers to reflect on what they have learned, their perceptions of the program and the value they would place on the program.

The Space Travelers complete the Observatorium self-reflection activity, responding to questions specific to what they have learned throughout the eight-mission journey. The Space Travelers select one of the things they learned and share it with the guests during the introductory phases of the Touchdown Party (i.e., when you introduce them to the guests).

OBSERVATORIUM cont.

☙ What are three helpful things you learned about during the *Space Travelers* program?

1. _____

2. _____

3. _____

☙ List four words that best describe the *Space Travelers* program. Make sure that each word means something different.

1. _____ 2. _____

3. _____ 4. _____

☙ Imagine you have been asked to e-mail a friend or classmate to tell him or her about what you learned during the *Space Travelers* program. What would you say?

Dear _____

_____

_____

_____

_____

☙ Which was your favorite mission? _____

_____

☙ What activities did you enjoy the most? _____

_____

☙ Would you recommend the *Space Travelers* program to other students? _____

_____

☙ Other comments: _____

_____

_____

_____

_____

SPACE TRAVELERS

SPACE GRADUATION CERTIFICATE

SPACE TRAVELER

Congratulations on successfully completing the Space Travelers program!

_____
Signature of Space Guide

___/___/___
(date)

MOTHER SHIP UPDATE

MISSION 8

Hello Parents/Guardians,

This is your final Mother Ship Update. If you have any questions, please do not hesitate to contact me. My contact information is as follows:

Name: _____

Phone: _____

Fax: _____

E-mail: _____

MISSION 8

The goal for Mission 8 was for the Space Travelers to reflect on their space journey and to celebrate what they had learned.

MISSION OUTCOMES

Students:

🌏 Reviewed the social understanding gained during the space journey

🌏 Celebrated working together as a crew during the space journey

🌏 Shared the social understanding they had learned during the space journey

Constellation Chart

MISSION 1
LAUNCH PAD

MISSION 5
ATMOSPHERIC PRESSURE

MISSION 2
INTRODUCING THE CREW

MISSION 6
MISSION CONTROL

MISSION 3
STARLIGHT AND GRAVITY THINKING

MISSION 7
SPACE WALKING – PREPARING FOR LANDING

MISSION 4
THE FEELINGS SHUTTLE

MISSION 8
TOUCHDOWN PARTY

125

SPACE TRAVELER'S JOURNAL

Date: _____

What I liked about today's mission:

New ideas I have learned:

What interested me most:

I'm curious about:

Actions I'm going to take:

SPACE GUIDE'S JOURNAL

This journal is completed by the Space Guide at the end of each mission to identify what went well with the mission, what was problematic, what was unexpected, what would be done differently if the mission was taught again, what questions came up during the mission, and so on.

Date: _____

What went well:

What was problematic:

What was unexpected:

What I would do differently if I taught this mission again:

What questions were raised for me during this mission:

Additional comments:

SPACE TRAVELERS' AUTOGRAPHS

Space Travelers invite members of their crew to sign their autographs on the Space Travelers' autographs page in their manual.

SUGGESTED READINGS

Many of the ideas behind the strategies and activities presented in this book have been inspired by the following.

Adderley, A., Petersen, L., & Gannoni, A. (1997). *Stop, think, do. Social skills training. First three years of schooling.* Melbourne, Australia: Australian Council for Educational Research.

Ammes, C. (1992). Classroom: Goals, structures and student motivation. *Journal of Educational Psychology, 84,* 261-271.

Andrews, J. (1992, May). Promoting positive peer relations. *Young Children,* 51-55.

Attwood, A. (1998). *Asperger's Syndrome: A guide for parents and professionals.* Philadelphia, PA: Jessica Kingsley Publishers.

Baker, J. E. (2003). *Social skills training for children and adolescents with Asperger Syndrome and social-communication problems.* Shawnee Mission, KS: Autism Asperger Publishing Company.

Bernard, M. (1992). *You can do it too!* Melbourne, Australia: Australian Scholarship Group.

Bernard, M., Linscott, J., & Nicholson, J. (1995). *Program achieve. Grades 3 and 4.* Melbourne, Australia: Australian Scholarship Group.

Bernard, M., Linscott, J., & Nicholson, J. (1995). *Program achieve. Grades 5 and 6.* Melbourne, Australia: Australian Scholarship Group.

Bernard, M., & Cartwrigth, M. (1995). *Program achieve. Grades 7 & 8.* Melbourne, Australia: Australian Scholarship Group.

Bodine, R., & Crawford, D. (1999). *Developing emotional intelligence.* Champaign, IL: Research Press.

Buron, K. D. (2003). *When my autism gets too big! A relaxation book for children with autism spectrum disorders.* Shawnee Mission, KS: Autism Asperger Publishing Company.

Buron, K. D., & Curtis, M. (2003). *The incredible 5-point scale – Assisting students with autism spectrum disorders in understanding social interactions and controlling their emotional responses.* Shawnee Mission, KS: Autism Asperger Publishing Company.

Callan, K. (1995). *Brave talk! Songs and activities to teach social skills to young children.* Narangba, Queensland, Australia: Calbar Publications.

Callan, K. (1995). *More brave talk!* Narangba, Queensland, Australia: Calbar Publications.

Cardon, T. (2004). *Let's talk emotions: Helping children with social cognitive deficits, including AS, HFA, and NVLD, learn to understand and express empathy and emotions.* Shawnee Mission, KS: Autism Asperger Publishing Company.

Carlebach, D., & Diekmann, C. (1999). *Peace scholars.* Miami, FL: Peace Education Foundation.

Carter, M. A. (2004). *Behaviour teaching and learning in educational settings. Not just surviving, definitely thriving.* Brisbane, Australia: M A Carter Consultancy.

Cellitti, A. (1998, Spring). Teaching peace concepts to children. *Dimensions of Early Childhood, 20-22.*

Cooper, M., & Griffith, K. (2000, March-April). The heart and soul of inclusion: Preparing classmates to care. *Autism-Asperger's Digest, 18-22.*

Denham, S. (1998). *Emotional development in young children.* London: Guilford Press.

Faherty, C. (2000). *Asperger's ... What does it mean to me? A workbook explaining self-awareness and life lessons to the child or youth with high functioning autism or Asperger's.* Arlington, TX: Future Horizons.

Faupel, A., Herrick, E., & Sharp, P. (1998). *Anger management.* London: David Fulton Publishers.

Fuller, A., Bellhouse, B., & Johnson, G. (2001). *The heart masters. A program for the promotion of emotional intelligence and resilience in the middle to senior years of primary schools.* Victoria, Australia: G. N. and E. J. Ridgway Publishers.

Gibbs, J. (1994). *Tribes. A new way of learning together.* Windsor, CA: Center Source Publications.

Goldstein, A. (1988). *The prepare curriculum. Teaching prosocial competencies.* Champaign, IL: Research Press.

Gray, C. (2000). *Gray's guide to bullying. Part 1: The basics.* Volume 12, No. 4. Jenison, MI: Jenison Public School and The Gray Center for Social Learning and Understanding.

Gray, C. (2001). *Gray's guide to bullying. Part 11: The real worlds.* Volume 13, No. 1. Jenison, MI: Jenison Public School and The Gray Center for Social Learning and Understanding.

Hale, J. (1991). *Friendship.* Melbourne, Australia: Hawker Brownlow Education.

Harrold, J. (1999). *Health. Levels 1-7. Developing awareness of health and personal development.* Balcatta, Western Australia: R.I.C. Publications.

HeartMath LLC, (2002). *The inside story – Understanding the power of feelings.* Boulder Creek, CA: Institute of HeartMath.

Heinrichs, R. (2003). *Perfect targets: Asperger Syndrome and bullying; Practical solutions for surviving the social world.* Shawnee Mission, KS: Autism Asperger Publishing Company.

Hill, S. (1997). *Games that work.* Armalade, Australia: Eleanor Curtain Publishing.

Huggins, P. (1994). *Teaching cooperation skills.* Colorado Springs, CO: Sopris West.

Huggins, P., Wood Manion, D., & Shakarian, L. (1998). *Helping kids handle put-downs.* Colorado Springs, CO: Sopris West.

Jasmine, J. (1998). *Conflict resolution. Years K-4.* Melbourne, Australia: Hawker Brownlow Education.

McAfee, J. (2002). *Navigating the social world.* Arlington, TX: Future Horizons.

McGrath, H. (1997). *Dirty tricks. Classroom games for teaching social skills.* Melbourne, Australia: Addison Wesley Longman Australia.

McGrath, H., & Noble, T. (1993). *Different kids, same classroom.* Melbourne, Australia: Longman Cheshire Ltd.

Myles, B.S., & Southwick, J. (1999). *Asperger Syndrome and difficult moments: Practical solutions for tantrums, rage, and meltdowns.* Shawnee Mission, KS: Autism Asperger Publishing Company.

New Zealand Police Youth Education Service. (1996). *Kia kaha. A resource kit about bullying for students, teachers and parents.* Wellington, New Zealand: New Zealand Police Youth Education Service.

Rizzo, S., Berkley, D., & Cozen, K. (1997). *Peacemaking skills for little kids.* Miami, FL: Peace Education Foundation, Inc.

Santomauro, J. (1999). *Set for gold – Strategies for life.* Brisbane, Australia: Author.

Schmidt, F., & Friedman, A. (1995). *Creative conflict solving for kids 5.* Miami, FL: Peace Education Foundation.

Schroeder, A. (1998). *Socially speaking. A pragmatic social skills program for pupils with mild to moderate learning disabilities.* Wisbech, Cambridgeshire: Learning Development Aids.

Wagner, S. (1998). *Inclusive programming for elementary students with autism.* Artlington, TX: Future Horizons.

Winner, M. (2002). *Thinking about you, thinking about me. Philosophy and strategies to further develop the perspective taking and communication abilities for person's with social cognitive deficits.* San Jose, CA: Author.

OTHER SOCIAL SKILLS RESOURCES PUBLISHED BY AAPC:

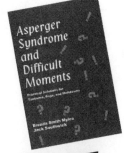

Asperger Syndrome and Difficult Moments:
Practical Solutions for Tantrums, Rage, and Meltdowns
Brenda Smith Myles and Jack Southwick

When My Autism Gets Too Big!
A Relaxation Book for Children with Autism Spectrum Disorders
Kari Dunn Buron; foreword by Brenda Smith Myles

Perfect Targets: Asperger Syndrome and Bullying;
Practical Solutions for Surviving the Social World
Rebekah Heinrichs

The Incredible 5-Point Scale – Assisting Students with Autism
Spectrum Disorders in Understanding Social Interactions and
Controlling Their Emotional Responses
Kari Dunn Buron and Mitzi Curtis

Let's Talk Emotions: Helping Children with Social Cognitive
Deficits, Including AS, HFA, and NVLD, Learn to Understand and Express
Empathy and Emotions
Teresa A. Cardon

Social Skills Training for Children and Adolescents
with Asperger Syndrome and Social-Communication Problems
Jed E. Baker

Joining In! A Program for Teaching Social Skills
Created by: Linda Murdock and Guru Shabad Khalsa
(Video)

AΛPC Autism Asperger
Publishing Company

In the US: To order, call **913-897-1004**, fax to **913-681-9473**
visit our website at **www.asperger.net** or mail to **AAPC • P.O. Box 23173 Shawnee Mission, KS 66283-0173**

Contact Book In Hand, for Australian prices and orders: Phone: **(07) 3885 8525**, Fax: **(07) 3885 8526**
visit the website at **www.bookinhand.com.au** or mail to **Book In Hand • P.O. Box 899, Redcliffe, Queensland 4020 AUSTRALIA**

NAME _____

ADDRESS _____

CITY _____

STATE ____ ZIP _____

PHONE _____

EMAIL _____

CODE	TITLE	PRICE	QTY.	TOTAL
9901a	Asperger Syndrome and Difficult Moments	$19.95		
9935	When My Autism Gets Too Big!	$15.95		
9936	The Incredible 5-Point Scale	$18.95		
9934	Let's Talk Emotions	$24.95		
9924	Social Skills Training	$34.95		
9918	Perfect Targets: Asperger Syndrome and Bullying	$21.95		
9701	Joining In! A Program for Teaching Social Skills (Video)	$79.95		

SHIPPING AND HANDLING/USA

Order Total	Ground
$1 – $50	$5
$51 – $100	$8
$101 – $200	$10
$201 – $300	$20
$301 – $400	$30
Over $400	$40

For rush, international or Canadian deliveries, please call toll-free 1-877-277-8254.

METHOD OF PAYMENT
☐ AMEX ☐ VISA ☐ DISCOVER ☐ MASTERCARD ☐ P.O. ATTACHED
☐ CHECK/MONEY ORDER ENCLOSED (PAYABLE TO AAPC)
ACCOUNT #

EXP. DATE [ ][ ]—[ ][ ] SIGNATURE _____

SUBTOTAL $ _____
7.5% KS SALES TAX + _____
(Kansas Residents Only)
SHIPPING & HANDLING + _____
TOTAL _____

(Required to process your order)